Table of Contents

Chapter 1: Introduction to AI 1
1.1 What is Artificial Intelligence? 3
1.2 Why AI Matters in Schools and Communities? 8
1.3 AI for Social Good 10
1.4 Generative AI and Large Language Model in Everyday Life 12
1.5 Practice Session 15

Chapter 2: AI-Powered Schools and Curriculum 19
2.1 Basics of IoTs, Immersive Technologies, Cloud, and Quantum Computing 21
2.2 Setting Up an AI Lab 26
2.3 AI Algorithms and Systems to Solve Problem 28
2.4 Integrating AI into the Curriculum 30
2.5 AI to Solve Practical Problems 31
2.6 Online AI Training and Virtual AI Lab 32
2.7 Practice Session 36

Chapter 3: AI in Everyday Academic Life 39
3.1 AI for Personalized Learning 41
3.2. AI for Time Management and Productivity 42
3.3. AI and Digital Literacy 43
3.4 Practice Session 44

Chapter 4: AI for Social Challenges 51
4.1 Addressing Family Challenges with AI 53
4.2 AI for Climate and Environmental Solutions 55
4.3 Community Development Through AI 55
4.4 Practice Session 57

Chapter 5: Innovation and Entrepreneurship with AI 63
5.1 Becoming an AI Innovator 65
5.2 AI-Powered Business Skills 66
5.3 Exploring AI Career Opportunities 67
5.4 Practice Session: Innovation and Entrepreneurship with AI 68

Chapter 6: Hands-On Activities and Exercises 73
6.1 Beginner-Level AI Projects 75
6.2 Problem-Solving Challenges 76
6.3 AI Competitions and Hackathons 76
6.4 Collaborative Group Activities 77

- 6.5 Creative AI Projects 78
- 6.6. Real-World Applications of AI Projects 78
- 6.7 Practice Session 79

Chapter 7: Empowering Teachers to Lead AI Initiatives 85
- 7.1 Training Teachers in AI Basics 87
- 7.2 Teaching AI Ethics and Safety 88
- 7.3 Continuous Professional Development 88
- 7.4 Facilitating AI Integration Across Subjects 89
- 7.5 Supporting Teachers in Leading AI Projects 90
- 7.6 Encouraging Teacher-Led AI Initiatives 90
- 7.7 Practice Session 91

Chapter 8: Building a community of AI Innovators 97
- 8.1. Engaging Families and Local Leaders 99
- 8.2 Showcasing Success Stories 100
- 8.3 Collaborating Across Communities 101
- 8.4 Encouraging Peer-to-Peer Learning 102
- 8.5 Promoting a Culture of Innovation 102
- 8.6 Practice Session 103

Chapter 9: Ethical Considerations in AI 109
- 9.1 Fairness and Inclusivity in AI 111
- 9.2 Data Privacy and Security 112
- 9.3 Responsible AI Development 113
- 9.4 Practice Session 114

Chapter 10: AI for National and Global Growth 121
- 10.1. Connecting Local Innovations to National Goals 123
- 10.2 AI as a Driver of Economic Growth 124
- 10.3 Building a Future-Ready Workforce 125
- 10.4 Scaling AI Innovations Globally 126
- 10.5 Promoting Ethical AI Practices for National Growth 126
- 10.6 Practice Session 127

Appendix – A 135

Appendix – B 143

AI in Schools

Build an AI-Powered Future for Schools, Families, and Communities

Prof Alamgir Hossain BSc, MSc, PhD, PgCe, MIEEE
CEO, Digital Readiness & Intelligent Systems Ltd, Durham, UK
Former Professor of AI & Head of Research Institutes/centres at
Universities (UK), Chairman of CSE (DU, Bangladesh), &
Vice President of CamTech Universitty (Cambodia).

Copyright © 2024 Prof Dr Alamgir Hossain

All rights reserved.

ISBN: 9798303261709

Preface

The dawn of artificial intelligence (AI) marks a transformative era for education, where the synergy of technology, innovation, and collaboration can empower schools, families, and communities like never before. "AI in Schools: Build an AI-Powered Future for Schools, Families, and Communities" is a guiding light for educators, policymakers, and learners, aiming to redefine the role of education in an AI-driven world.

This book stems from the profound belief that AI is not merely a tool but a partner in addressing the challenges of the 21st century. With its potential to personalize learning, enhance teaching strategies, and solve societal issues, AI invites us to envision schools as hubs of innovation where technology and human ingenuity come together. By exploring its applications in achieving Sustainable Development Goals (SDGs), fostering innovation, and addressing community challenges, this work bridges the gap between education and real-world impact.

The narrative unfolds with a clear purpose: to empower educators with practical strategies to integrate AI into curricula, inspire students to harness its potential, and unite communities in collaborative problem-solving. With accessible explanations, case studies, and exercises, the book ensures that readers not only understand AI but can actively implement its benefits in their daily lives.

As you embark on this journey, I invite you to explore the possibilities, challenge the conventions, and embrace the transformative power of AI. Let this book inspire you to lead change in your classrooms, communities, and beyond, building a future where technology serves humanity with compassion, equity, and creativity.

Abstract

AI is revolutionizing education, presenting unprecedented opportunities to enhance learning, teaching, and community engagement. This book explores the transformative potential of AI, offering a comprehensive roadmap for integrating AI technologies into educational environments.

The book examines into foundational concepts of AI, practical applications in schools, and its role in addressing societal challenges such as healthcare, climate change, and economic development. By bridging technical insights with real-world case studies, it empowers educators to implement AI-driven tools for personalized learning, optimize teaching methods, and prepare students for future-ready careers.

Through interdisciplinary approaches and actionable strategies, the book highlights the critical importance of collaboration among schools, families, and communities in leveraging AI for Sustainable Development Goals (SDGs). Practical exercises, innovative project ideas, and ethical considerations provide readers with a robust framework to harness AI responsibly and effectively.

Designed for educators, students, policymakers, and community leaders, this book inspires a collective vision of schools as innovation hubs where AI fosters equity, creativity, and global problem-solving. It is both a guide and a call to action to build an AI-powered future that benefits all.

Please use LLMs, such as ChatGPT, to expand on any guideline provided in the book for better understanding by using the guideline text as a prompt.

Acknowledgment

I extend my heartfelt gratitude to the diligent research assistants and esteemed colleagues whose invaluable contributions made this book possible. Dr. Lokman Khan, Mr. Hesam Rostamali, and Ms. Yashashvi Basha have been instrumental in shaping the comprehensive resource that **"AI in Schools: Build an AI-Powered Future for Schools, Families, and Communities"** aspires to be. Their expertise, dedication, and insights greatly enriched the depth and scope of this work.

I would also like to express my sincere appreciation for the language models ChatGPT, Gemini, Claude, and other advanced large language models (LLMs), whose assistance was pivotal throughout the preparation of this book. Their ability to augment human efforts underscores the potential of AI to enhance knowledge creation and dissemination.

This book reflects the combined strength of human intellect and cutting-edge AI technology, ensuring it serves as a valuable guide for educators, policymakers, families, and communities alike. Together, these collaborations embody the spirit of innovation and shared purpose that this work seeks to promote.

Chapter 1:
Introduction to AI

1.1 What is Artificial Intelligence?

Artificial Intelligence (AI) is a branch of computer science that enables machines to perform tasks that typically require human intelligence. These tasks include learning, reasoning, problem-solving, and understanding language. Unlike traditional computer systems that follow specific instructions, AI systems can **learn from data**, adapt to new information, and improve their performance over time.

In addition to human intelligence, **nature-inspired intelligence** plays a significant role in solving complex problems by mimicking patterns and behaviours observed in nature. For example, **ant colony optimization**—inspired by the way ants find the shortest path to food—has been applied to solve logistical challenges such as optimizing delivery routes and network traffic management. By studying and replicating the efficiency of natural systems, researchers develop innovative algorithms (step-by-step actions to perform tasks) and solutions for real-world issues.

Figure 1.1: Human Intelligence and Nature Inspired Intelligence

Importance of AI:

AI is reshaping our world by **enhancing services, increasing productivity, and reducing processing time and costs**. It monitors and automates tasks, improves decision-making and drives innovation. From personalized experiences to solving complex global problems, AI is a powerful tool that is transforming our lives. By embracing AI responsibly, we can unlock its potential for a better future.

While survival without AI might be possible in some fields, flourishing and growing in your profession will likely require at least a basic understanding of AI. The **earlier you adopt and adapt to AI**, the more you'll future-proof your career and open-up opportunities for innovation and success.

Figure 1.2: AI generated prediction

Though AI is a relatively new field, there has been a surge in experts and professionals well-versed in AI technologies. This growing pool of expertise assists businesses in selecting the most suitable AI solutions for their specific needs and effectively implementing them (Source: Harvard Business Review).

Primary Types of AI for Users:

Generative AI is more tangible and visible, as it directly produces creative content like text, images, videos and code. It's the AI that powers tools like ChatGPT, Gemini and Claude.

General AI, on the other hand, is a more theoretical concept of AI that can understand or learn any intellectual task that a human being can. It's the kind of AI often depicted in science fiction, capable of independent thought and problem-solving.

Difference Between General AI and Generative AI:

Aspect	General AI	Generative AI
Definition	General Artificial Intelligence (AGI) refers to AI systems with the capability to perform any intellectual task that a human can do, exhibiting generalized problem-solving skills and adaptability.	Generative AI is a subset of AI focused on creating content, such as text, images, audio, or video, based on learned patterns in data.
Scope of Functionality	Broad and versatile; designed to understand and execute a wide range of tasks across multiple domains.	Specialized; primarily focused on generating new content or simulations in specific domains like natural language or visual art.
Core Capability	Mimics human intelligence comprehensively, with reasoning, learning, and problem-solving across tasks.	Creates new data (e.g., text, images) that resembles the input it was trained on.
Development Stage	Still theoretical and under research; AGI has not been fully realized or implemented.	Actively in use, technologies like GPT, DALL·E, and Stable Diffusion are examples of generative AI systems.
Examples	Hypothetical systems like an AI capable of learning any task humans can perform at a human level or beyond.	Applications like ChatGPT (for text), DALL·E (for images), and music generation tools like OpenAI Jukebox.
Use Cases	Potentially unlimited; could handle complex, multi-disciplinary tasks like medical diagnosis, scientific research, and autonomous decision-making.	Content creation, creative industries, chatbots, personalized marketing, and enhancing simulations or training datasets.
Adaptability	Highly adaptable; intended to learn and perform tasks it has never encountered before.	Limited adaptability; requires training data and functions within the scope of its trained domain.
Focus	Focuses on replicating human-like intelligence and decision-making holistically.	Focuses on producing original content or simulating realistic outputs within its trained scope.

In essence, **General AI** aims to emulate the breadth and depth of human intelligence across domains, while **Generative AI** is a narrower application of AI, excelling in creating specific types of content within its training framework.

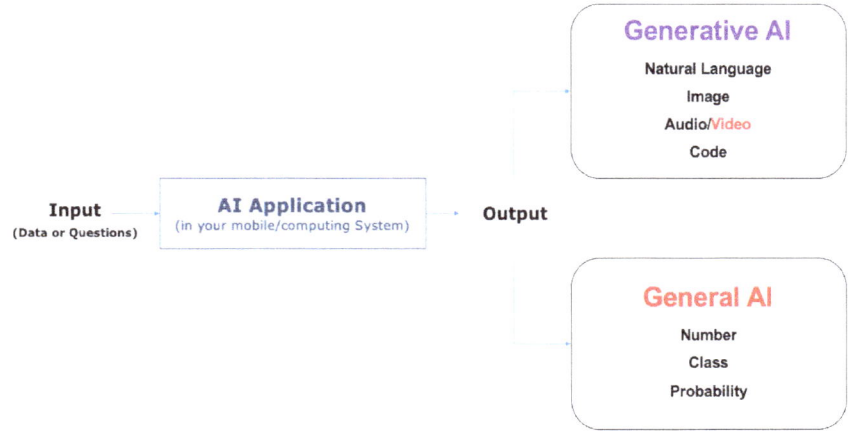

Figure 1.3: Basic Model of Generative and General AI system

Key Features of AI:
- **Machine Learning (ML)**: The ability of machines to learn from data without explicit programming.
- **Natural Language Processing (NLP)**: Understanding and generating human language.
- **Computer Vision**: Recognizing and interpreting visual data like images and videos.
- **Automation**: Performing repetitive tasks efficiently and accurately.

Real-Life Examples of AI in Action:
- **Smart Assistants:** AI-powered tools like Siri, Alexa, and Google Assistant help answer questions, set reminders, and control smart devices.
- **Personalized Recommendations:** Online platforms like Netflix and YouTube use AI to suggest content based on user preferences.

- **Healthcare Applications:** AI tools assist doctors by analysing medical images or predicting disease risks.
- **Agriculture:** AI systems monitor soil health, weather conditions, water conditions and crop growth, optimizing farming practices.
- **Education:** Intelligent tutoring systems provide personalized learning experiences for students.

1.2 Why AI Matters in Schools and Communities?

AI matters in schools and communities because it enhances learning through personalized education, automates routine tasks for teachers, and empowers students with future-ready skills. Additionally, it addresses community challenges such as healthcare, agriculture, and resource management, driving innovation and improving quality of life.

Figure 1.4: AI-Lab at School to Work with Communities to Address SDGs Challenges

(SDGs stands for Sustainable Development Goals. They are a collection of 17 global goals set by the United Nations in 2015. These goals aim to address global challenges like poverty, inequality, climate change, environmental degradation, peace, and justice.)

How AI Transforms Learning, Teaching, and Everyday Problem-Solving?
- **For Students**:
  - AI-powered tools personalize learning by adapting to each student's pace and style, making education more effective.
  - AI simplifies research by providing quick access to relevant information, knowledge and insights.
  - Students can use AI to enhance creativity, such as generating ideas for projects or improving writing skills.
- **For Teachers**:
  - AI automates repetitive tasks like grading assignments, freeing up time for interactive teaching.
  - AI tools can analyse student performance and identify areas where additional support is needed.
  - Teachers can use AI to create engaging lesson plans and learning activities.
- **For Communities**:
  - AI-powered solutions address local challenges, such as improving healthcare access or monitoring water quality.
  - Small businesses can use AI for better financial planning, market analysis, and customer engagement.

AI's Role in Preparing Students for the Future of Work and Innovation:
- **Workforce Readiness:**
  - AI is becoming a critical component of industries like healthcare, agriculture, finance, and education. Learning AI skills prepares students for high-demand careers in these fields.
  - Students with AI knowledge are better equipped to adapt to rapidly changing job markets.

- **Fostering Innovation:**
    - AI empowers students to think creatively and develop solutions for real-world problems.
    - With AI, students can explore entrepreneurship opportunities, turning their innovative ideas into impactful businesses.

1.3 AI for Social Good

AI for Social Good leverages technology to solve critical societal challenges, such as using AI-powered diagnostic tools to improve healthcare access in underserved areas or optimizing farming practices to combat food insecurity. Additionally, AI helps monitor climate change impacts and supports disaster management, enabling proactive measures to protect lives and the environment.

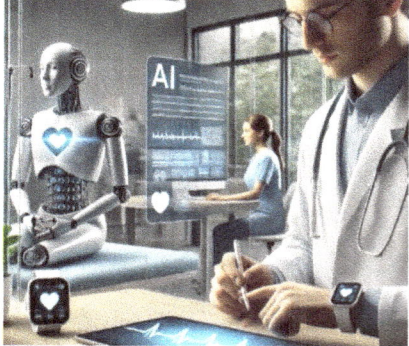

Figure 1.5: Practical Scenario to Address the Challenges using AI

How AI Addresses Local and Global Challenges?

AI has immense potential to solve pressing social issues, both locally and globally:

- **Agriculture**: AI helps farmers optimize crop yields, conserve water, and reduce resource wastage.
- **Healthcare**: AI aids in early disease detection, personalized treatment plans, and telemedicine, making healthcare more accessible and affordable.

- **Education**: AI bridges gaps in education by providing inclusive learning opportunities for marginalized communities.
- **Climate Change**: AI-powered systems monitor environmental changes, predict natural disasters, and promote sustainable energy practices.
- **Infrastructure**: Smart cities use AI to manage traffic, conserve energy, and improve public services efficiently.

Success Stories of AI-Powered Solutions in Various Fields:

- **Agriculture**:
  - AI tools like sensors and drones are used in Bangladesh to monitor crop health and suggest optimal harvesting times, boosting productivity.
- **Healthcare**:
  - AI-based diagnostic systems like IBM Watson assist doctors in analysing complex medical data, leading to faster and more accurate diagnoses.
- **Education:**
  - Duolingo, an AI-powered language learning app, personalizes lessons based on user progress, making language learning accessible worldwide.
- **Climate Action:**
  - AI-driven satellite imagery is used to monitor deforestation and predict weather patterns, enabling proactive measures against climate change.
- **Disaster Management**:
  - AI models forecast natural disasters like floods and cyclones, helping communities prepare and minimize damage.

1.4 Generative AI and Large Language Model in Everyday Life

What are Generative AI and Large Language Models?
As indicated earlier, generative AI is a type of artificial intelligence that can create new content, like text, images, audio and video. Think of it as a super-powered tool that can help you with your schoolwork and creative projects.

Large Language Models (LLMs) are a type of artificial intelligence that is trained on massive amounts of text data. They are designed to understand and generate human language, making them capable of tasks like translation, summarization, and creative writing. Examples: ChatGPT.com, Gemini.google.com, Calude.ai, etc. You can use image, audio, and video generation tools in conjunction with LLMs as add-ons to enhance the output and create more comprehensive content.

Prompt for Generative AI:
1. A prompt is a specific instruction or query given to a Large Language Model (LLM) to generate text.
2. Prompts are crucial as they guide the LLM's response, determining the quality, relevance, and creativity of the output.
3. When a prompt is provided, the LLM processes the input, accesses its vast knowledge base, and generates text that aligns with the prompt's intent.
4. Effective prompting involves using clear and concise language, providing specific instructions, and considering the desired tone and style of the output.
5. Well-crafted prompts can unlock the full potential of LLMs, enabling them to generate insightful, informative, and engaging text.

Prompt for image, audio and video generation:
You can write prompts for image, audio, and video generation. Here are some examples:

Image Generation Prompts:
- **Specific Image:** " Create an image of a beautiful rural village in Bangladesh". See the response of this prompt in Figure 1.6.
- **Artistic Style:** "A portrait of a robot in the style of Van Gogh, oil painting, vibrant colours, dramatic lighting"
- **Conceptual:** "A surreal dreamscape with a giant eyeball floating in the sky, hyper-realistic, 4K resolution"

Audio Generation Prompts:
- **Music:** "A melancholic piano melody, minor key, slow tempo, inspired by Chopin"
- **Sound Effect:** "A spooky, eerie sound effect, like a creaking door in a haunted house"
- **Voiceover:** "A deep, authoritative voice reading a news report about climate change, urgent tone"

Video Generation Prompts:
- **Short Film:** "A sci-fi short film about a lone astronaut exploring a distant planet, cinematic, suspenseful, dramatic music"
- **Animated Video:** "A cute, animated video about a friendly robot helping a child with homework, colourful, upbeat, child-friendly"
- **Explainer Video:** "A simple explainer video about how to use a new app, clear, concise, step-by-step"

Remember, the more specific and detailed your prompt, the better the AI model can understand your vision and generate the desired output. Experiment with different prompts and styles to achieve your desired results.

*Figure 1.6: Response to the prompt
'Create an image of a beautiful rural village in Bangladesh'*

*Figure 1.7: Prompt
'Create a beautiful image of a girl playing a keyboard near majestic mountains, capturing the serene atmosphere and the joy of music in nature'.*

Figure 1.8: Prompt
'Create a serene and picturesque scene featuring a charming house nestled by a glistening lake, surrounded by a lush and vibrant garden. Let your imagination paint a tranquil and inviting setting that exudes beauty and tranquillity'

1.5 Practice Session

Exercise 1. Text Generation

- **Brainstorming Ideas:** Use AI writing tools like Rytr or Jasper (formerly Jarvis) to generate creative writing prompts or topic suggestions.
- **Research Assistance:** Employ AI-powered research tools to quickly gather information and cite sources.
- **Drafting and Editing:** Utilize AI writing assistants to draft initial drafts and suggest improvements in grammar, style, and clarity.

Use Gemini.Google.com (or Other Generative AL tool) and ask the question: *I am good at mathematics. What are some potential career opportunities I can consider after my university studies?*

- **Replace the subject:** Replace "Mathematics" with a subject you love, such as "History," "Art," or "Biology."

- **Ask the question:** Formulate a question related to your chosen subject. For example, if you love history, you might ask, "I am fascinated by history. What are some potential career opportunities I can consider after my university studies?"
- **Learn:** Research the potential career paths and educational requirements associated with your chosen field.
- **Write an Essay** using multiple prompts for 3 A4 pages

Exercise 2. Image Creation
- **Image Generation:** Use tools like Midjourney or Stable Diffusion to create stunning images based on your text descriptions.
- **Image Editing:** Employ AI-powered tools like Adobe Photoshop's Neural Filters to enhance images, remove imperfections, or create artistic effects.

Use Microsoft Co-Pilot or any other image-generating tools. Insert the prompt *'Create a housing model with a nice river view beside the house'* to get the response. It may offer one like the image below. Write a prompt to create the one you like with a garden, garage, river view beside it, etc.

Figure 1.9: Images Created by AI with Simple Questions

Exercise 3: Investigative Task

Explore the topic: "**How can I, as a student, contribute to mitigating climate change?**" Use different LLMs to explore variations in their responses to this prompt.
- **Provide context:** Include your location, region, and country to make the essay relevant to your specific environment.
- **Write a brief report:** Prepare a 3-page A4 report summarizing your findings.
- **Create a presentation:** Develop a 10-minute presentation to share your insights with the team.

By following these guidelines and utilizing the capabilities of different LLMs, you can gain valuable insights and develop innovative solutions to address climate change.

This chapter introduces the foundational concepts of artificial intelligence (AI) and its relevance to education and communities. AI is defined as a field of computer science that enables machines to perform tasks requiring human-like intelligence, including learning, problem-solving, and decision-making. It explores types of AI, such as Generative AI for creating content and General AI, a theoretical model for broader intellectual tasks. The chapter highlights AI's transformative potential to enhance learning, streamline teaching, and address community challenges, while emphasizing the need for responsible integration to foster innovation and prepare for a digital future. students and educators for a rapidly evolving digital world.

Chapter 2:
AI-Powered Schools and Curriculum

AI-Powered Schools and Curriculum explores how integrating AI into education can transform the way students learn, and teachers teach. By establishing **AI labs** and embedding AI tools into various subjects, schools can create engaging, personalized learning experiences while equipping students with essential future skills. This chapter provides practical strategies for setting up AI resources, incorporating AI-driven activities and fostering innovation through curriculum alignment, ensuring that education evolves to meet the demands of a rapidly changing world.

2.1 Basics of IoTs, Immersive Technologies, Cloud, and Quantum Computing

The integration of advanced digital technologies such as the Internet of Things (IoT), immersive technologies, cloud computing, and quantum computing with Artificial Intelligence (AI) is transforming the way schools, families, and communities address practical challenges. Understanding these technologies is essential for fostering a future-ready education system that equips students with the skills needed to solve real-world problems innovatively.

The Internet of Things (IoT): Connecting the World

The Internet of Things refers to a network of physical devices connected through the internet, capable of collecting, sharing, and analysing data. These devices include sensors, smart home gadgets, and wearables.

IoT and AI Integration

IoT devices generate vast amounts of data, which AI can analyse to extract meaningful insights. This combination is crucial for real-time monitoring conditions (for example, condition of water in a fish pond) decision-making and automation.

Applications in Schools

- **Smart Classrooms**: IoT-enabled devices like smartboards, temperature sensors, and automated lighting systems create more efficient learning environments. AI analyses data from these devices to optimize energy use and student comfort.
- **Student Safety**: IoT-based attendance systems combined with AI can monitor student location and ensure safety on school premises.
- **Health Monitoring**: Wearable devices in schools track student activity levels, and AI processes this data to promote healthier habits.

Practical Challenges Solved

- **Resource Optimization**: IoT helps manage school resources like electricity and water by using AI to identify wastage and suggest solutions.
- **Attendance and Engagement**: AI-powered IoT attendance systems track student participation and suggest interventions for absenteeism.

Immersive Technologies: Enhancing Learning Experiences:

Immersive Technologies

Immersive technologies, such as Virtual Reality (VR), Augmented Reality (AR), and Mixed Reality (MR), create highly interactive and engaging digital environments that simulate real-life scenarios.

Immersive Technologies and AI Integration

AI enhances immersive experiences by personalizing content, recognizing user behaviour, and adapting learning modules based on performance.

Applications in Schools
- **Virtual Field Trips**: AR/VR tools allow students to explore historical sites, scientific labs, or ecosystems from the classroom. AI customizes these experiences to suit individual learning needs.
- **Skill Development**: AI-powered VR simulations enable students to practice real-world skills, such as coding, surgery, or mechanical repairs, in a safe environment.
- **Inclusive Learning**: Immersive technologies support students with disabilities by providing interactive and accessible content tailored to their needs.

Practical Challenges Solved
- **Learning Engagement**: Immersive experiences driven by AI keep students more engaged and motivated to learn.
- **Complex Concept Visualization**: AR/VR simplifies abstract or complex subjects, such as physics experiments or chemical reactions, through interactive simulations.

Cloud Computing: Accessing AI Anytime, Anywhere:

Cloud Computing
Cloud computing provides on-demand access to computing resources, such as storage, processing power, and applications, over the internet. It eliminates the need for expensive hardware and infrastructure.

Cloud Computing and AI Integration
AI systems require vast amounts of data and computational power, which the cloud provides. Cloud platforms like Google Cloud, AWS, and Azure enable schools to access AI tools without heavy infrastructure investments.

Applications in Schools
- **E-Learning Platforms**: Cloud-based systems like Google Classroom and Khan Academy integrate AI to provide personalized learning experiences.
- **Collaboration Tools**: Students and teachers collaborate on cloud-based platforms like Microsoft Teams, with AI-driven features such as real-time transcription and content suggestions.
- **Data Management**: Cloud systems securely store student data, enabling AI to analyse performance trends and recommend improvements.

Practical Challenges Solved
- **Cost Reduction**: Cloud computing reduces the need for expensive on-premises infrastructure.
- **Scalability**: Schools can easily expand AI-driven tools and applications as their needs grow.

Quantum Computing: Unlocking Unprecedented AI Power:

Quantum Computing
Quantum computing is a cutting-edge technology that uses quantum mechanics principles to process complex computations far faster than traditional computers.

Quantum Computing and AI Integration
Quantum computing enhances AI capabilities by solving complex problems, such as optimization and large-scale data analysis, which traditional systems struggle with.

Applications in Schools
- **Advanced Problem-Solving**: Quantum-enhanced AI tools can solve complex scheduling problems, such as optimizing class timetables or resource allocation.
- **Research and Innovation**: Students can access quantum-powered simulations to explore fields like physics, biology, and chemistry.
- **Real-Time Data Processing**: Quantum AI enables faster analysis of massive datasets, such as school-wide performance or environmental monitoring data.

Practical Challenges Solved
- **Optimization Problems**: Schools can use quantum AI to optimize transportation routes, minimizing time and costs.
- **Advanced Curriculum**: Quantum computing introduces students to next-generation technologies, preparing them for high-demand careers.

The Importance of Integration:

Integrating IoT, immersive technologies, cloud computing, and quantum computing with AI has transformative potential in solving real-world challenges.

Key Benefits:
1. **Efficiency**: AI-driven IoT and cloud solutions streamline operations in schools and communities.
2. **Accessibility**: Immersive technologies democratize education by making learning engaging and inclusive.
3. **Innovation**: Quantum computing powers cutting-edge research and problem-solving.
4. **Scalability**: Cloud-based AI tools make it easier to expand and implement solutions across multiple schools and communities.

Educators, students, and communities must embrace these technologies, understanding their synergy with AI to build a sustainable and innovative future. By leveraging the basics of IoT, immersive technologies, cloud computing, and quantum computing, schools can become hubs of transformative learning and problem-solving for the 21st century.

2.2 Setting Up an AI Lab

Requirements for a basic AI Lab: Tools, Software, and Infrastructure:
An AI lab can start with just a good smartphone, access to some free AI tools, and a good internet connection. However, setting up a standard AI lab requires the following essential components:

- **Hardware**
    - Computers or laptops with sufficient processing power.
    - IoT devices like sensors, cameras, and microcontrollers (e.g., Raspberry Pi, Arduino).
    - Robotics kits for hands-on AI experimentation.
- **Software**
    - AI platforms and tools like Google Colab, TensorFlow, or Scratch for beginner-friendly programming.
    - Data visualization tools like Tableau or Excel for teaching data analysis.
    - Educational AI apps and platforms tailored to student learning levels.

Figure 2.1: AI-Lab in School – students with communities

- **Learning Materials:**
  - Handbooks, online courses, and guides on AI basics, machine learning, and data science.
  - Pre-designed project templates for classroom use.

- **Space and Infrastructure:**
  - A dedicated ventilated room equipped with seating, whiteboards, and projectors.
  - Adequate power supply and backup systems for uninterrupted sessions.

Role of Teachers, Students, and the Community in Using AI Labs Effectively:

- **Teachers**
  - Facilitate AI learning by designing curriculum-aligned projects and guiding students in experiments. Use ChatGPT and Gemini for guidance to do that.
  - Act as mentors, ensuring students understand ethical AI usage and the practical applications of AI concepts.

- **Students**
  - Use the lab for hands-on learning, creating AI-powered projects that address real-life challenges.
  - Collaborate with peers to innovate solutions, fostering teamwork and creativity.

- **Community**
  - Engage parents and local leaders in AI projects to ensure community support.
  - Use the lab to develop AI-driven solutions for local issues, making the lab a resource hub for the community.

2.3 AI Algorithms and Systems to Solve Problem

AI Algorithms:

An algorithm is a well-defined, step-by-step procedure or set of rules designed to solve a specific problem or perform a particular task. AI algorithms are the core computational processes that enable machines to mimic human intelligence by solving problems, recognizing patterns, learning from data, and making decisions. These algorithms form the foundation of artificial intelligence systems, powering applications such as image recognition, natural language processing, and robotics. The way algorithm works:

- **Input Data**: The algorithm receives data, such as images, text, or numerical values.
- **Processing**: The algorithm applies mathematical models or statistical techniques to analyse the data.
- **Learning**: Based on the input, the algorithm adjusts its parameters to improve accuracy or efficiency.
- **Output**: The algorithm produces a result, such as a prediction, classification, or decision.

AI algorithms are the backbone of artificial intelligence, enabling machines to learn, adapt, and make decisions across a wide range of applications. Understanding these algorithms helps us harness their power responsibly to create innovative solutions for real-world challenges.

Algorithms and Systems:

A system is a set of interconnected components that function together to achieve a specific goal. The relationship between an algorithm and a system can be understood as the role that the algorithm plays in the overall functioning and organisation of the system. A system is typically a collection of interrelated components or processes working together to achieve a specific goal or to perform a particular function. In the context of computing or information systems, these components may include hardware, software, data, and people.

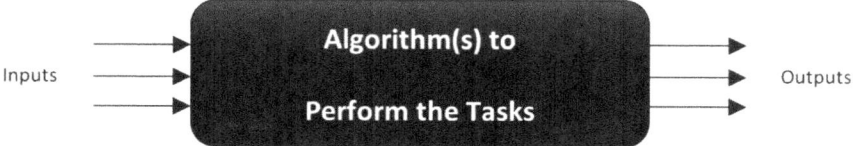

Figure: 2.2: Open Loop Multi-inputs and Multi-output System

An algorithm serves as a fundamental building block within a system, providing the logic and rules for processing information, making decisions, or executing specific tasks. It is an essential part of the software component of the system. The system uses algorithms to achieve its goals efficiently and accurately, while the algorithms themselves rely on the system's resources (e.g., memory, processing power, input/output devices) to execute their operations.

Figure 2.2, 2.3 and 2.4 shows three different commonly used systems. Understanding feedback look and reinforcement models are essential terminologies to read this book.

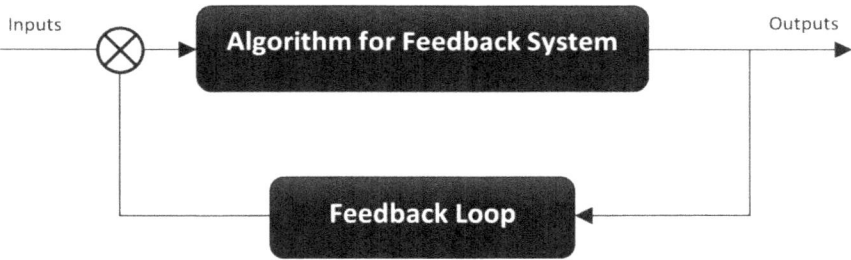

Figure 2.3: Feedback Systems to Adjust with Target Outputs

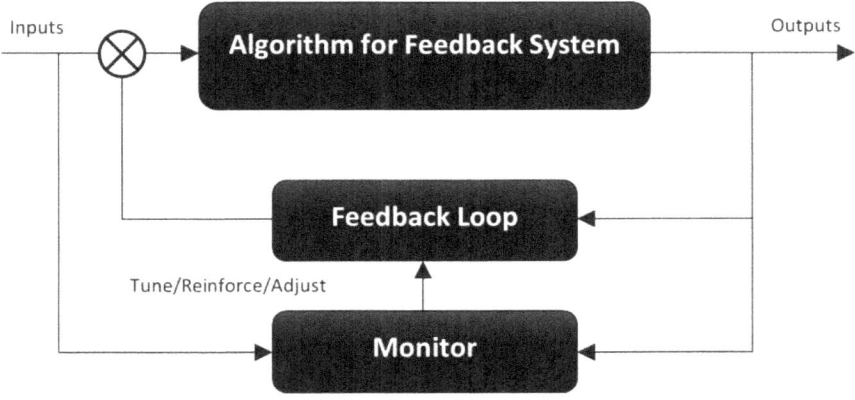

Figure 2.4: Dynamic Adaptive System through Reinforcing Feedback Parameters

2.4 Integrating AI into the Curriculum

Subject-Specific Applications of AI

- **Science:**
  - Use AI to analyse data from experiments (e.g., measuring environmental changes or chemical reactions).
  - Simulate systems like weather patterns or the human body.
- **Mathematics**
  - Teach AI concepts like pattern recognition and predictive modelling using mathematical principles.
  - Use AI tools for data visualization and statistical analysis.
- **Literature and Language:**
  - AI-powered tools like Grammarly help improve writing skills.
  - Language translation apps introduce students to diverse cultures and languages.
- **Arts:**
  - AI-generated art and music platforms inspire creativity and innovation.
  - Use AI tools for design, animation, and storytelling projects.
- **Social Studies:**
  - Teach students how AI is used to analyse historical data and predict societal trends.
  - Explore AI applications in governance, urban planning, and disaster management.

AI-Driven Activities, Projects, and Learning Exercises

- Design interactive quizzes and games using AI to make learning engaging.
- Develop AI-based projects, such as chatbots to answer curriculum-related questions or AI programs to solve real-life problems.
- Conduct collaborative AI challenges, where students work in groups to create AI solutions for local issues.

2.5 AI to Solve Practical Problems

Using AI to Tackle Community Challenges
- **Agriculture**:
  - Use AI-powered tools to monitor crop health, optimize irrigation, and predict weather patterns.
  - Implement IoT devices in farms to provide real-time data for decision-making.
- **Education:**
  - AI can analyse attendance and performance data to identify students needing additional support.
  - Intelligent tutoring systems provide personalized learning experiences.
- **Healthcare:**
  - AI-driven health monitoring tools can assist in diagnosing common illnesses.
  - Telemedicine platforms powered by AI enable remote consultations and medical support.

Case Studies of Successful AI Applications in Local Problem-Solving
- **Agriculture:**
  - In rural Bangladesh, IoT sensors combined with AI were used to predict soil moisture levels, reducing water wastage by 30%.
- **Education:**
  - A school in India implemented AI tutoring systems that improved student performance by 20% in math and science.
- **Healthcare:**
  - AI diagnostic tools helped a community clinic in Africa reduce patient wait times by 50% by triaging cases based on urgency.
- **Climate Action:**
  - AI-powered drones in Indonesia monitored deforestation rates, enabling timely reforestation efforts.

2.6 Online AI Training and Virtual AI Lab

There are numerous online resources available to help beginners learn about AI. Here are some of the best options, including YouTube channels and online courses:

YouTube Channels:
- **3Blue1Brown:** This channel offers excellent visual explanations of complex mathematical concepts, including those related to machine learning and neural networks.
  Link:
  https://www.youtube.com/c/3blue1brown
- **Sentdex:** This channel provides practical tutorials on Python programming and machine learning, with a focus on hands-on projects.
  Link:
  https://www.youtube.com/channel/UCfzlCWGWYyIQ0aLC5w48gBQ
- **StatQuest with Josh Starmer:** This channel provides clear and concise explanations of statistical concepts, including those relevant to machine learning.
  Link:
  https://www.youtube.com/channel/UCtYLUTtgS3k1Fg4y5tAhLbw
- **Machine Learning with Jason:** This channel offers a variety of machine learning tutorials, from beginner to advanced levels.
  Link:
  https://machinelearningmastery.com/5-free-youtube-channels-dedicated-to-machine-learning-education/

Online Courses:
- **Coursera:** This platform offers a wide range of machine learning courses, from introductory to advanced levels. Some popular options include:
  - Machine Learning by Andrew Ng

- o Machine Learning Specialization by Stanford University
- o Deep Learning Specialization by Andrew Ng
- **edX:** This platform also offers a variety of machine learning courses, including:
  - o Machine Learning by Columbia University
  - o MicroMasters Program in Statistics and Data Science from MIT
- **Udacity:** This platform offers a variety of machine learning nanodegrees, including:
  - o Machine Learning Engineer Nanodegree
  - o Artificial Intelligence Nanodegree
- **Kaggle:** This platform offers a variety of machine learning courses and competitions, which can help you learn by doing.
  Link:
  https://commons.wikimedia.org/wiki/File:Kaggle_logo.png

Other Resources:

- **Google's Machine Learning Crash Course:** This free online course provides a comprehensive introduction to machine learning.
  Link:
  https://medium.com/@shubhanshugupta/my-learning-experience-with-googles-machine-learning-crash-course-bd9a033213c3
- **Fast.ai:** This platform offers free online courses and resources for learning deep learning.
  Link:
  https://forums.fast.ai/t/hello-new-student-with-fastpages-blog/95419
- **Machine Learning Mastery:** This website offers a variety of machine learning tutorials and courses, including a free machine learning course for beginners.
  Link:
  https://machinelearningmastery.com/

Additional Tips:
- **Start with the basics:** Make sure you have a solid understanding of the fundamentals of machine learning, such as linear algebra, calculus, and probability theory.
- **Practice, practice, practice:** The best way to learn machine learning is to practice. There are many online resources available to help you get started, such as Kaggle and GitHub.
- **Don't be afraid to ask for help:** There are many online communities where you can ask questions and get help from other machine learning enthusiasts.
- **Stay up to date:** Machine learning is a rapidly evolving field, so it's important to stay up to date with the latest trends and technologies.

Virtual AI Lab:

There are several virtual AI labs available for beginners to learn and experiment with AI concepts:

Microsoft AI for Beginners:
- This GitHub repository offers a comprehensive, hands-on introduction to AI, covering topics like computer vision, natural language processing, and machine learning. It includes Jupyter Notebooks for practical exercises.
- Link: https://microsoft.github.io/AI-For-Beginners/

Google's Machine Learning Crash Course:
- This free online course provides a comprehensive introduction to machine learning, with interactive exercises and real-world examples.
- Link: https://developers.google.com/machine-learning/crash-course

Kaggle:
- While primarily a platform for data science competitions, Kaggle offers a variety of datasets, notebooks, and tutorials for beginners to practice machine learning and AI.
- Link: https://www.kaggle.com/

Google Colab:
- This free cloud-based Jupyter notebook environment allows you to run Python code directly in your browser, making it ideal for experimenting with machine learning and AI.
- Link: https://colab.research.google.com/

Amazon SageMaker:
- This fully managed platform from Amazon Web Services provides a range of tools and services for building, training, and deploying machine learning models. It offers a free tier for beginners to get started.
- Link: https://aws.amazon.com/sagemaker/

Paperspace:
- This cloud-based platform provides virtual machines with powerful GPUs, making it ideal for training complex machine learning models. It offers a free trial for beginners to experiment.
- Link: https://www.paperspace.com/

Additional Tips:
- **Start with the basics:** Make sure you have a solid understanding of Python programming and linear algebra before diving into AI.
- **Practice regularly:** The best way to learn AI is by doing. Experiment with different techniques and datasets.
- **Join online communities:** Engage with other AI learners on forums like Reddit, Stack Overflow, and Kaggle.
- **Take advantage of online courses and tutorials:** There are many excellent online courses and tutorials available to help you learn AI.
- **Don't be afraid to make mistakes:** AI is a complex field, and it's okay to make mistakes. Learn from your mistakes and keep experimenting.

By leveraging these resources and following these tips, you can start your journey into the world of AI.

2.7 Practice Session

Exercise 1: Deep Dive into Your Interests with LLMs
Leverage Large Language Models (LLMs) to explore your areas of interest and enhance your skills. Choose one/more of the tasks below or create your own topic to investigate:
- **Enhancing Programming Skills:**
    - Write a detailed prompt to find free resources to improve your programming skills.
    - Use the responses to locate top-rated YouTube tutorials, free coding platforms, or beginner-friendly programming communities.
- **Freelancing Opportunities:**
    - Create a prompt to explore freelancing opportunities in your chosen field.
    - Gather information on essential skills, popular platforms (e.g., Upwork, Fiverr), and tips to build a freelancing portfolio.
- **Fisheries and Technology:**
    - Draft a prompt to learn about monitoring fish farming using sensors.
    - Research the environmental conditions (e.g., pH levels, temperature) required for specific fish species.
- **Health Monitoring for Diabetes:**
    - Write a prompt to understand how AI can assist in diabetes monitoring and lifestyle management.
    - Investigate tools and techniques that help track glucose levels and optimize diets.
- **Predicting Food Prices in Extreme Weather:**
    - Develop a prompt to analyse food price predictions under unusual weather conditions, such as flooding.
    - Use historical data and AI tools to estimate how reduced production affects prices, focusing on staples like rice.

- **Choose Your Own Adventure:**
    o Think of a topic you're passionate about and create a prompt to explore it deeply.
    o Share what you've learned with your classmates!

Exercise 2: Investigative Task

Explore the topic: "How can AI be used to analyse prescription patterns, identify overprescribing, and detect potential conflicts of interest?"
- **Use different LLMs:** Explore variations in their responses to this prompt.
- **Provide context:** Include your location, region, and country to make the essay relevant to your specific environment.
- **Write a brief report:** Prepare a 3-page A4 report summarizing your findings.
- **Create a presentation:** Develop a 10-minute presentation to share your insights with the team.

By following these guidelines and utilizing the capabilities of different LLMs, you can gain valuable insights and develop innovative solutions to improve healthcare practices and patient safety.

Other Ideas:
- Suggest ways to optimize local agriculture.
- Identify opportunities for eco-friendly small businesses.
- Explore AI-driven approaches to improve healthcare or education in your community. For example, use the prompt:

'*Create a visual 3D model of the human body with blood circulation*' and see the model as shown in Figure 2.5.

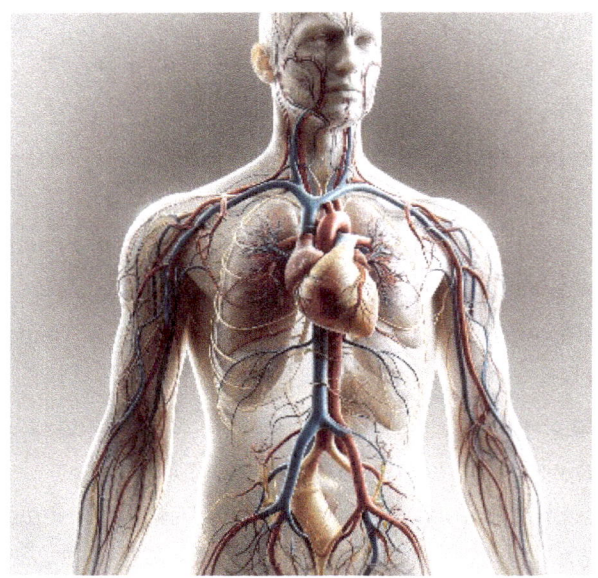

Figure 2.5: An Image of 3D Human Body with Blood Circulation

Chapter 2 explores how integrating AI into schools can revolutionize education by transforming learning experiences and teaching methods. It discusses the role of AI-powered tools in personalizing education, fostering innovation, and addressing real-world challenges through interdisciplinary approaches. The chapter highlights the importance of establishing AI labs, utilizing technologies like IoT, immersive tools, and cloud computing, and aligning curricula with AI-driven activities to prepare students for future careers. Emphasis is placed on equipping educators and students with the resources and skills to implement AI solutions effectively and collaboratively within schools and communities.

Chapter 3:
AI in Everyday Academic Life

AI in Everyday Academic Life highlights how AI can enhance the daily routines of students and teachers, making learning more efficient and personalized. From AI-powered tools that tailor education to individual needs to apps that improve time management and productivity, this chapter explores practical applications of AI in academics. By integrating AI into study habits and digital literacy, students and teachers can unlock new possibilities for growth, creativity, and success in their educational journey.

3.1 AI for Personalized Learning

Tools for Tailoring Education to Individual Needs
AI-powered tools adapt learning experiences based on each student's abilities, pace and preferences:

- **Intelligent Tutoring Systems (ITS)**: Platforms like Khan Academy and Duolingo provide personalized lessons and instant feedback to help students learn at their own pace.
- **Adaptive Learning Software**: Tools such as Dream Box and Prodigy analyse student performance and adjust the difficulty level of lessons to ensure continuous progress.
- **AI-Powered Assessments**: Online platforms offer tailored quizzes and exercises, identifying strengths and areas for improvement for each student.

Enhancing Study Habits Using AI-Powered Apps

AI applications help students improve study efficiency and effectiveness:
- **Study Planners**: AI apps like MyStudyLife and Trello organize study schedules, setting reminders for assignments and exams.
- **Learning Assistants**: Tools like Quizlet use AI to create custom flashcards and practice tests, reinforcing knowledge retention.
- **AI Note-Taking Tools**: Apps like Otter.ai transcribe and summarize lectures, making it easier for students to review and revise key concepts.

3.2. AI for Time Management and Productivity

Managing academic responsibilities becomes simpler and more efficient with AI-powered tools:
- **Calendar and Task Management Apps**: Tools like Google Calendar and Todoist help students plan their daily activities, prioritize tasks, and avoid procrastination.
- **Smart Reminder Systems**: AI-driven apps send alerts for approaching deadlines and scheduled study sessions.
- **Virtual Study Buddies**: Platforms like Forest and Focus@Will use gamification and productivity music to keep students focused while studying.

Figure 3.1 Style of AI-enable Learning Expecting under AI-Lab

Examples of practical AI tools:
- **AI Timetable Generators**: Create personalized timetables that allocate time-based on subject difficulty and student priorities.
- **Collaboration Tools**: AI-powered platforms like Slack and Microsoft Teams streamline group assignments, enabling effective teamwork.

3.3. AI and Digital Literacy

Navigating Digital Platforms Responsibly and Effectively:
As digital technologies become central to education, understanding how to use them responsibly is crucial:
- **Safe Online Practices**: AI-powered browsers and tools like Safe Search ensure students access reliable and appropriate information.
- **Digital Etiquette**: Teaching students how to interact respectfully and responsibly in virtual classrooms and online forums.
- **AI-Powered Search Engines**: Tools like Bing AI and Wolfram Alpha help students efficiently find accurate information for assignments and projects.

Understanding the Role of Data in Everyday AI Applications:
Data plays a significant role in powering AI tools, and understanding its importance is essential:
- **Data Collection**: AI systems analyse data from user inputs (e.g., learning habits, preferences) to personalize experiences.
- **Data Privacy**: Teaching students to protect their personal information by using secure platforms and understanding terms of service agreements.
- **Ethical Use of Data**: Helping students recognize the importance of using data responsibly and understanding how it impacts AI decision-making processes.

Practical examples:
- **Fitness and Health Apps**: AI-based tools like MyFitnessPal demonstrate how data collection helps create personalized health plans.
- **AI in E-Commerce**: Understanding how platforms like Amazon use purchase data to suggest products teaches students real-world applications of AI.

3.4 Practice Session

This practice session explores the role of AI in enhancing your daily academic routines, helping you develop personalized learning habits, improve time management, and build digital literacy skills.

Exercise 1: Exploring AI for Personalized Learning
Task:
- Select one of the following AI-powered tools or methods and try it out:
    1. **Intelligent Tutoring Systems**: Use platforms like **Khan Academy** or **Duolingo** for a subject you want to improve.
    2. **Adaptive Learning Software**: Try tools like **Dream Box** or **Prodigy** and observe how the lessons adapt to your progress.
    3. **AI Note-Taking Tools**: Record a lecture or summarize a reading using **Otter.ai** or a similar app.

Reflect:
Write a short note about how the AI tool made learning easier or helped you understand a topic better.

Exercise 2: Enhancing Study Habits with AI
Task:
- Pick one of these AI-powered apps and use it for a day:
    1. **MyStudyLife** or **Trello**: Create a study schedule and track your tasks.
    2. **Quizlet**: Make a set of flashcards for an upcoming test or quiz, and test yourself using the app.

3. **Focus@Will** or **Forest**: Use these tools to stay focused during study sessions.

Reflect:
Did the app improve your productivity? What features were most helpful?

Exercise 3: AI for Time Management and Productivity
Task:
- Use an AI-powered calendar tool like **Google Calendar** or **Todoist** to organize your schoolwork and personal commitments.
  - Set reminders for assignments, deadlines, and upcoming exams.
  - Create a weekly timetable using an AI timetable generator.

Reflect:
How did organizing your tasks with AI change your approach to managing your time?

Exercise 4: Building Digital Literacy with AI
Task:
- Explore **Safe Search** or **Wolfram Alpha** to find information for a school project.
- Use AI responsibly by following these steps:
  - Check if the website or tool is secure.
  - Look for ethical and accurate sources of information.
  - Avoid plagiarism by summarizing ideas in your own words.

Try this: Write the prompt to Gemini.Google.com: *'To buy an online product, what should I check to know whether the site is secure?'*
You may have a response like the one below. Explore each of these steps to understand online shopping:
"Here are some key things to check before making an online purchase:
1. Secure Connection:
- **HTTPS:** *Ensure the website URL starts with "https://". The "s" indicates a secure connection.*

- **Lock Icon:** Look for a padlock icon in the address bar. This signifies a secure connection.

2. **Website Trustworthiness:**
   - **SSL Certificate:** Check for a valid SSL certificate, often indicated by a green padlock or a trust seal.
   - **Website Reviews:** Read reviews from other customers to gauge the website's reputation.
   - Contact Information: Verify the website's contact information, including a physical address and phone number.

3. **Payment Security:**
   - **Secure Payment Gateways:** Use reputable payment gateways like PayPal or Stripe.
   - **Avoid Public Wi-Fi:** Be cautious when making online purchases on public Wi-Fi networks.

4. **Privacy Policy:**
   - **Read the Privacy Policy:** Understand how the website collects, uses, and protects your personal information.
   - **Data Privacy:** Ensure the website complies with data privacy regulations like GDPR or CCPA.

Additional Tips:
   - **Use Strong Passwords:** Create strong, unique passwords for your online accounts.
   - **Be Wary of Phishing Attempts:** Avoid clicking on suspicious links or downloading attachments from unknown sources.
   - **Use a Reliable Antivirus:** Keep your device protected with reputable antivirus software.

By following these guidelines, you can significantly reduce the risk of online fraud and protect your personal information."

Reflect:

What did you learn about using AI tools responsibly? Did the tool help you find reliable information faster?

Exercise 5: Understanding Data in AI Applications

Task:

- Think of one app or tool you use frequently (e.g., fitness apps, e-commerce sites like Amazon).
    - Research how it uses data to personalize your experience.
    - Discuss why data privacy is essential and how you can protect your personal information while using these tools.

Try this: Write the prompt to Gemini.Google.com: *'What steps can I take to ensure the genuineness of a person I'm communicating with on Facebook?'* You may have a response like the one below:

"Here are some steps to verify the authenticity of someone on Facebook:

1. *Check the Profile:*
    - *Look for a verified badge: A blue checkmark indicates that Facebook has verified the account.*
    - *How to get verified on Facebook: Your step-by-step guide - Sprout Social; Link: https://sproutsocial.com/*
    - *Examine the profile picture and cover photo: Are they clear and consistent with the person's identity?*
    - *Review the "About" section: Does the information provided seem accurate and consistent with the person's online presence?*
2. *Mutual Friends:*
    - *See if you have mutual friends who can vouch for the person's identity.*
3. *Video Chat:*
    - *Initiate a video call to see the person's face and hear their voice.*
4. *Reverse Image Search:*
    - *Use Google Image Search to check if the profile picture is used elsewhere online.*
5. *Be Cautious and Trust Your Instincts:*
    - *If something seems suspicious or too good to be true, it probably is.*
    - *Avoid sharing personal information with people you don't know well.*

Remember, online relationships can be deceptive, so it's important to exercise caution and use common sense.

Reflect:

Write a short paragraph on how data impacts AI's effectiveness and your role in using data responsibly.

Exercise 6: Investigative Task

Topic: My school's academic curriculum focuses on science. How can I use my educational skills to solve community problems?

Instructions:

- **Research Using AI Tools:**
    - Utilize various large language models (LLMs), such as ChatGPT, Bard, or similar platforms, to explore different ways science-based educational skills can address community issues.
    - Compare responses from different LLMs to understand the diversity of ideas and approaches.
- **Provide Context for Relevance:**
    - Tailor your research to your specific environment by providing context, such as:
        - Your **area of interest** (e.g., environmental science, health, or technology).
        - **Location** and **region**, focusing on challenges faced by your community.
        - The **country**, emphasizing cultural, social, or economic factors that influence the problems and solutions.
- **Identify Potential Community Problems:**
    - Use your science education to explore real-world challenges in your community. Examples include:
        - Environmental issues like waste management or pollution.
        - Public health concerns such as lack of clean drinking water or spread of diseases.

- Technology access gaps in rural areas.
- Educational inequalities or lack of STEM resources.
- **Analyse Practical Solutions:**
  - Input the prompt into LLMs and gather ideas on how to apply your educational skills to solve these problems.
  - Explore approaches such as:
    - Creating science-based awareness campaigns.
    - Developing low-cost, locally implementable technologies.
    - Using data-driven methods to analyse and address issues.
- **Write a Report:**
  - Prepare a concise report (3 A4 pages) summarizing your findings. Include the following sections:
    - Introduction: Describe the importance of using science skills to solve community problems.
    - Methodology: Explain how LLMs and contextual research were used.
    - Findings: Highlight key solutions suggested by LLMs and their relevance to your community.
    - Discussion: Analyse how these solutions can be implemented locally, including potential challenges.
    - Recommendations: Provide actionable steps for using your educational skills to create positive change.
- **Prepare a Presentation:**
  - Create a 10-minute presentation based on your report.
  - Include visuals, such as diagrams, charts, or case study examples, to illustrate your points.
  - Structure the presentation to:
    - Introduce the community problems.
    - Showcase how science-based skills can address these challenges.
    - Conclude with recommendations and next steps.

Deliverables:
1. **Written Report:**
    o A 3-page document detailing your research, findings, and recommendations.
2. **Slide Deck:**
    o A 10-minute presentation with visuals and concise explanations of your findings.

Goal:

This exercise encourages you to leverage your science education to address real-world challenges, while gaining insights from AI tools to develop practical, community-focused solutions. It also enhances your ability to present and implement these solutions effectively within your local context.

Chapter 3 highlights how AI enhances daily academic routines for students and teachers by making learning more efficient, personalized, and engaging. It explores AI-powered tools like intelligent tutoring systems, adaptive learning software, and virtual assistants that tailor education to individual needs while improving productivity through time management apps. The chapter also emphasizes the importance of digital literacy, teaching students to use AI responsibly and navigate online platforms effectively. By integrating AI into study habits, schools can unlock new opportunities for creativity, growth, and success in education.

Chapter 4:
AI for Social Challenges

AI for Social Challenges explores into how AI can be a powerful tool for addressing pressing issues in communities, such as improving agriculture, enhancing healthcare, and tackling environmental concerns. This chapter explores practical applications of AI, empowering students and communities to use technology to find innovative solutions to local and global problems. By leveraging AI for social good, students can develop impactful projects that create meaningful change and contribute to sustainable development.

4.1 Addressing Family Challenges with AI

AI offers practical solutions to address common family challenges in agriculture, healthcare, and financial planning:

- **AI in Agriculture for Better Farming:**
  - AI-powered tools analyse soil health, weather patterns, and crop conditions to optimize farming practices.
  - Smart irrigation systems reduce water wastage by providing precise watering schedules.
  - AI-based pest detection tools help farmers protect crops efficiently without overusing chemicals.
  - Example: A farmer uses an AI-powered mobile app to predict the best planting time, leading to higher crop yields and reduced resource wastage.

- **AI for Health Monitoring:**
  - Wearable devices like Fitbits and smartwatches monitor heart rates, physical activity, and sleep patterns, providing insights into family health.
  - AI-based telemedicine platforms allow families in remote areas to consult doctors and access medical advice without travelling.
  - Chatbots powered by AI offer instant answers to health-related queries, ensuring timely interventions.
  - **Example:** A mother uses an AI app to track her child's vaccination schedule, receiving timely reminders and health advice.
- **AI for Financial Planning:**
  - AI-driven budgeting tools like Mint analyse income and expenses, helping families manage their finances effectively.
  - Investment platforms powered by AI suggest personalized savings plans and investment strategies.
  - **Example:** A family uses an AI app to create a monthly grocery budget and track expenses, reducing unnecessary spending.

Figure 4.1: AI for Agriculture and Healthcare

4.2 AI for Climate and Environmental Solutions

AI is a powerful tool for promoting climate-friendly solutions and protecting the environment:

- **Waste Management:**
    - AI-powered systems identify recyclable materials and sort waste efficiently.
    - Smart bins equipped with sensors and AI alert waste collectors when full, reducing litter and pollution.
    - **Example:** A community uses AI-enabled waste sorting machines to improve recycling rates and minimize landfill waste.
- **Energy Efficiency:**
    - AI optimizes energy consumption in homes and businesses by adjusting heating, cooling, and lighting based on usage patterns.
    - Smart grids powered by AI predict energy demand and distribute electricity efficiently, reducing energy wastage.
    - **Example:** A school uses an AI energy management system to monitor electricity use, cutting costs and promoting sustainability.
- **Environmental Monitoring:**
    - AI analyses satellite images and sensor data to monitor deforestation, air quality, and water pollution.
    - Predictive models powered by AI warn about natural disasters like floods, enabling early preparedness.
    - **Example:** A village uses AI-powered drones to monitor local forest health, preventing illegal logging and preserving biodiversity.

4.3 Community Development Through AI

Students can actively contribute to their communities by participating in AI-focused initiatives that address local needs:

- **Water Quality Testing:**
    - IoT sensors and AI analyses water samples for contamination, ensuring safe drinking water for families.
    - **Example:** Students conduct a project using AI-enabled devices to test local water sources, sharing results with the community and recommending solutions for clean water.
- **Renewable Energy Adoption:**
    - AI-powered solar energy systems track energy production and usage, optimizing renewable energy deployment.
    - **Example:** Students lead a project to install solar panels in a local community centre, using AI to monitor energy efficiency.
- **Agricultural Community Support:**
    - Students create AI models to predict crop diseases and share insights with local farmers, increasing agricultural productivity.
    - **Example:** A group of students develops a chatbot powered by AI that provides farmers with real-time weather forecasts and planting tips.
- **Climate Awareness Campaigns:**
    - AI tools analyses community energy consumption and suggest ways to reduce carbon footprints.
    - **Example:** Students use AI platforms to design posters and videos for campaigns promoting energy conservation and recycling.

Figure 4.2: AI's Role in Climate and Environmental Issues

4.4 Practice Session

This practice session focuses on how AI can address social and environmental challenges, improve family life, and empower communities. By exploring these real-world applications, you will learn how to use AI for positive change.

Exercise 1: AI in Daily Family Life
Task:
Explore how AI can solve common family challenges. Choose one of the scenarios below:

1. **Improving Farming with AI:**
   - Research an AI-powered tool or app that helps with farming tasks like soil analysis or pest detection.
   - Simulate its use by writing a plan for how it could help a local farmer improve crop yields.

2. **Health Monitoring:**
   - Use or explore a health-tracking app (e.g., Fitbit, Google Fit) to monitor daily activities like steps, sleep, or exercise.
   - Describe how these insights can benefit family health or help manage a specific health condition.

3. **Financial Planning:**
   - Test an AI budgeting tool (e.g., Mint or Goodbudget) by entering sample income and expenses.
   - Share how it helps in creating a monthly plan to save money and avoid overspending.

Exercice 2 : AI for Environnemental Solutions
Task:
Learn how AI contributes to climate and environmental sustainability. Choose one of these challenges to explore:

1. **Waste Management:**
   - Research AI-based waste sorting systems or smart bins.

- Propose how your school or community could implement one to improve recycling rates.
2. **Energy Efficiency:**
   - Analyse how AI optimizes energy use (e.g., smart thermostats or grids).
   - Create a plan for your school or home to adopt an AI-powered energy-saving device.
3. **Environmental Monitoring:**
   - Investigate how AI-powered tools monitor deforestation or water quality.
   - Write a scenario where such a tool helps solve an environmental issue in your local area.

Exercise 3: Community AI Projects
Task:
Work in groups to create an AI-driven solution for a community challenge. Select one of the following projects:
1. **Water Quality Testing:**
   - Simulate using AI tools to test local water sources for contamination.
   - Present your findings and suggest ways to ensure safe drinking water.
2. **Renewable Energy Installation:**
   - Design a project plan for installing solar panels in your school or community.
   - Use AI to track energy production and show the benefits of renewable energy.
3. **Agricultural Support:**
   - Build a simple chatbot or write prompts that give farmers real-time weather updates and planting advice.
   - Test your chatbot with mock queries to see how it can help local farmers.

4. **Climate Awareness Campaign:**
   - Use an AI design tool like Canva or ChatGPT to create posters or videos promoting recycling or energy conservation.
   - Share your campaign materials with classmates and discuss their impact.

Try This: Write a prompt to create a depiction of how the world will look (see figure 4.3 below) by 2050 based on weather conditions and analyse the context.

Figure 4.3: Predictive weather conditions in 2050

Exercise 4: Investigative Team Work Task

Topic: "How can an AI-powered drone help our agriculture?"

Instructions:

- **Research Using AI Tools:**
  - Utilize various large language models (LLMs) such as ChatGPT, Bard, or other similar platforms to explore how AI-powered drones can benefit agriculture.
  - Investigate the potential applications of drones in tasks like crop monitoring, pest control, irrigation management, and yield optimization.

- **Contextualize Your Research:**
    - Tailor your findings to a specific area of interest in agriculture (e.g., Mango farming, rice cultivation, or greenhouse management).
    - Incorporate details about your location, region, and country to make the report relevant to local agricultural practices and challenges.
- **Write a Report:**
    - Prepare a brief report (approximately 3 A4 pages) summarizing your findings.
    - Include the following sections:
        - **Introduction**: Outline the importance of AI-powered drones in agriculture.
        - **Applications**: Highlight specific ways drones can improve agricultural productivity.
        - **Challenges and Limitations**: Discuss potential barriers, such as cost, technical skills, or weather conditions.
        - **Recommendations**: Provide suggestions for implementing AI-powered drones effectively in your chosen context.
- **Prepare a Presentation:**
    - Create a 10-minute presentation based on your findings.
    - Use slides to emphasize:
        - Key applications of AI-powered drones in agriculture.
        - Examples specific to your chosen area of interest.
        - Benefits and challenges.

Deliverables:
1. **Written Report:**
   - A well-structured 3-page report covering:
     - Overview of AI-powered drones.
     - Practical applications in your area of agricultural interest.
     - Insights gained from different LLM responses.
     - Contextual analysis based on your location.
2. **Slide Deck:**
   - A 10-minute presentation with visuals, graphs, or images to enhance understanding.

Goal:

This exercise aims to develop an understanding of how AI-powered drones can revolutionize agriculture, address local challenges, and improve productivity. It also builds skills in contextual research, critical thinking, and team work effective communication.

Chapter 4 explores the role of AI in addressing pressing social challenges, focusing on areas such as agriculture, healthcare, and environmental sustainability. It highlights how AI-powered tools, like drones for crop monitoring, telemedicine platforms, and smart waste management systems, can create tangible benefits for communities. The chapter emphasizes the importance of student and community collaboration in leveraging AI to solve local and global issues, including achieving Sustainable Development Goals (SDGs). By showcasing real-world applications and success stories, it inspires readers to use AI innovatively and responsibly to drive positive social change.

Chapter 5:
Innovation and Entrepreneurship with AI

Innovation and Entrepreneurship with AI focuses on empowering students and communities to harness AI for creating innovative solutions and entrepreneurial ventures. This chapter explores how AI can spark creativity, drive problem-solving, and help transform ideas into impactful businesses that address real-world challenges. By developing AI-powered business skills and exploring career opportunities, learners can become future-ready innovators and entrepreneurs, contributing to economic growth and community transformation.

5.1 Becoming an AI Innovator

Encouraging Creative Thinking and Problem-Solving Through AI

AI enables students to approach problems with innovative and creative solutions:

- **Identifying Challenges**: Encourage students to observe real-life issues in their communities, such as resource wastage, traffic congestion, or lack of healthcare access.
- **Using AI Tools for Innovation**: Introduce tools like machine learning models, natural language processing, and computer vision to brainstorm and prototype solutions.
- **Collaborative Innovation**: Promote teamwork where students share ideas, develop models, and test solutions together.
  - **Example**: A group of students designs an AI app to help farmers predict the best time to plant crops based on weather data.

Turning Ideas into AI-Powered Solutions

- **Ideation to Prototyping**: Provide a step-by-step guide to turning concepts into functional AI tools, from identifying a problem to developing a prototype.

- **Testing and Refining**: Encourage students to use AI platforms like Google Colab or Microsoft Azure to refine their ideas and create user-friendly solutions.
    - **Example**: A student designs a chatbot to help local businesses manage customer inquiries efficiently.

5.2 AI-Powered Business Skills

Introduction to Entrepreneurship and Building Startups Using AI

AI Entrepreneurship refers to the practice of using AI technologies to develop innovative businesses that address real-world problems. Entrepreneurs in this field identify specific challenges and apply AI tools and algorithms to create efficient, scalable, and impactful solutions.

- **Steps to Start an AI Business**:
    - Identify a market need.
    - Develop an AI-based solution.
    - Create a business plan.
    - Secure funding or partnerships.
- **Practical Skills for Entrepreneurs**:
    - Data analysis for identifying trends and customer preferences.
    - Marketing through AI-powered tools like predictive analytics.
    - Financial management using AI apps for budgeting and forecasting.

Case Studies of Youth-Led AI Businesses

- **Agriculture**: A student-led startup uses AI-powered drones to monitor soil conditions, helping farmers optimize fertilizer use.
- **Healthcare**: Young entrepreneurs develop an AI app for early detection of common illnesses using image recognition.
- **Education**: A school project evolves into a business that creates AI-powered personalized tutoring platforms.
    - **Example**: A teenager in India founded a company that uses AI to teach coding to children worldwide, earning recognition and revenue.

5.3 Exploring AI Career Opportunities

Overview of AI-Related Careers

AI is transforming every major industry, creating diverse career opportunities:

- **Agriculture**: AI specialists develop tools for precision farming, crop monitoring, and supply chain management.
- **Healthcare**: Careers include developing AI-powered diagnostics, health monitoring systems, and telemedicine platforms.
- **Education**: Opportunities involve creating AI learning platforms, intelligent tutoring systems, and educational analytics tools.
- **Technology**: Roles include AI developers, data scientists, and machine learning engineers, contributing to advancements in software, robotics, and automation.

Skills Needed to Succeed in AI-Driven Industries

- **Technical Skills**:
  - Programming languages like Python and R.
  - Understanding of machine learning, deep learning, and AI algorithms.
  - Familiarity with AI tools like TensorFlow, PyTorch, and cloud-based platforms.
- **Analytical and Creative Thinking**:
  - Ability to interpret data, identify patterns, and develop creative solutions.
- **Soft Skills:**
  - Effective communication, teamwork, and problem-solving abilities.
  - Ethical decision-making to ensure responsible AI usage.
- **Lifelong Learning:**
  - Staying updated with the latest AI technologies and trends through courses, workshops, and certifications.

5.4 Practice Session: Innovation and Entrepreneurship with AI

This practice session focuses on using AI to foster creativity, develop entrepreneurial skills, and explore exciting career opportunities. You will brainstorm innovative ideas, create prototypes, and understand how AI can drive businesses and careers.

Exercise 1: Becoming an AI Innovator

Task 1: Identify Challenges in Your Community
- Observe your surroundings and identify a real-life issue, such as:
    1. Resource wastage.
    2. Traffic congestion.
    3. Limited healthcare access.

Task 2: Brainstorm AI-Powered Solutions
- Think of how AI could solve the problem. Examples:
    - Use AI to predict traffic patterns and suggest alternative routes.
    - Create an app that tracks and reduces food waste in your school.

Task 3: Prototype Your Idea
- Sketch or describe how your AI-powered tool or app would work.
- Use platforms like **Google Colab** or **Microsoft Azure** to test simple prototypes (if feasible).

Exercise 2: AI-Powered Business Skills

Task 1: Develop an AI Business Plan
- Follow these steps to outline a business idea:
    - Identify a market need (e.g., farmers need better tools to predict weather).
    - Describe your AI-based solution (e.g., an app for real-time weather predictions).
    - Draft a simple business plan, including target users, funding ideas, and goals.

Task 2: Practical Entrepreneurship Skills

- Explore one of these tools:
  - **Data Analysis**: Use Google Sheets or Python to identify trends in a dataset.
  - **Marketing with AI**: Research how tools like Google Ads or predictive analytics help businesses find customers.
  - **Financial Management**: Try AI apps like Mint or Wally to create a sample budget for your business.

Exercise 3: Exploring AI Careers

Task 1: AI Career Exploration

- Choose an industry you are interested in (e.g., agriculture, healthcare, or technology).
- Research how AI is transforming this field. For example:
  - In healthcare, AI is used for diagnostics and telemedicine.
  - In education, AI powers personalized learning platforms.

Task 2: Skill Development Pathway

- Identify key skills required for a career in your chosen field:
  - Programming (e.g., Python).
  - AI tools (e.g., Tensor Flow).
  - Analytical thinking.
- Create a learning plan to develop one of these skills. For instance:
  - Watch a YouTube tutorial on Python basics.
  - Practice using a beginner AI tool like Teachable Machine.

Exercise 4: Collaborative Innovation Project

Task: Group Activity

- Form small groups to brainstorm and prototype an AI solution for a shared challenge.

Examples:
- o An app to reduce school food waste.
- o A chatbot to answer common student questions about exams.
- o A tool to help local businesses improve customer service using AI.
* Present your project idea to the class, including:
- o The problem you're addressing.
- o How AI solves it.
- o A simple sketch or description of your tool.

Exercise 5: Investigative Tasks

Topic: Exploring Plant Diseases Using AI-Powered Tools
Instructions:
* **Use AI Tools for Plant Disease Identification**:
  - o Provide a prompt to a large language model (LLM), such as ChatGPT or similar tools, along the lines of:
    "What are the different diseases in these images of plant leaves?"
  - o Attach or describe the image clearly in your prompt. If images cannot be directly analysed by the LLM, consider using AI-powered platforms designed for image analysis, such as Google Lens, Plantix, and Dr.chash (mobile app) alongside your text-based queries.

Figure 5.1: Images of plants with different diseases

- **Conduct Research**:
  - Explore how LLMs or AI-based platforms analyse symptoms and identify plant diseases.
  - Compare the responses from different tools and note any variations or consistencies in the diagnoses.
- **Analyse Contextual Relevance**:
  - Consider the location, type of crops, and specific environmental conditions (e.g., humidity, soil type, or pest prevalence) when interpreting the AI's output.
  - Reflect on how these factors influence plant diseases and AI diagnoses.
- **Write a Report**:
  - Prepare a concise report (approximately 2-3 A4 pages) summarizing your findings.
  - Include the following sections:
    - **Introduction**: Overview of plant diseases and the role of AI in their identification.
    - **Methodology**: Steps taken to use LLMs or AI tools for disease analysis.
    - **Findings**: List diseases identified from the images and insights from different LLM responses.
    - **Challenges**: Discuss limitations of using AI for this task, such as image quality or regional specificity.
    - **Conclusion**: Highlight the potential of AI tools in improving agricultural practices.
- **Prepare a Presentation:**
  - Create a 5-10 minute presentation summarizing your findings.
  - Include images, results, and a comparison of the AI tools' performance.

Deliverables:
1. **Written Report:**
   o A well-structured 3-page document detailing your findings and reflections.
2. **Presentation Slides:**
   o A concise slide deck (5-7 slides) with visuals to support your presentation.

Goal:

This exercise helps you explore how AI-powered tools, including LLMs, can assist in diagnosing plant diseases. By comparing tool outputs and reflecting on their effectiveness, you will better understand the practical applications and limitations of AI in agriculture.

Chapter 5 highlights the transformative potential of AI in fostering innovation and driving entrepreneurial ventures. It explores how AI tools can empower students and communities to identify challenges, brainstorm solutions, and create impactful startups addressing real-world problems. Practical guidance is provided on developing AI-powered business ideas, leveraging skills like data analysis and predictive modelling, and exploring diverse career opportunities in AI-driven industries. By showcasing success stories and emphasizing creativity, the chapter inspires readers to harness AI for economic growth and meaningful societal contributions.

Chapter 6:
Hands-On Activities and Exercises

Hands-on activities and Exercises provide practical opportunities for students to explore and apply AI concepts in real-world scenarios. This chapter includes beginner-level projects, collaborative problem-solving challenges, and creative exercises designed to inspire innovation and teamwork. By engaging in these activities, students will gain confidence in using AI tools, develop critical thinking skills, and contribute meaningful solutions to their schools and communities.

6.1 Beginner-Level AI Projects

Purpose: Introduce students to basic AI concepts and applications through simple, practical projects.

- **Creating a Chatbot**:
  - Use tools like Scratch, Python, or Dialog flow to build a chatbot that answers simple questions or provides information.
  - **Example**: A chatbot that helps students find study resources or school event schedules.
- **Analysing Weather Data**:
  - Students collect local weather data and use AI tools like Microsoft Excel or Google Colab to analyse patterns and predict conditions.
  - **Example**: A project that predicts rainfall for farming or school activities.
- **Building Simple AI Models:**
  - Use platforms like Teachable Machine or Weka to create image or sound recognition models.
  - **Example**: A model that identifies different types of fruits based on images.

6.2 Problem-Solving Challenges

Purpose: Encourage students to apply AI to address real-world problems within their community.

- **Improving School Attendance**:
  - Use AI tools to analyse attendance data and identify patterns causing absenteeism.
  - **Example**: Students create a notification system that reminds parents about their child's attendance status.
- **Monitoring Crop Health**:
  - Use drones or IoT devices to collect data on crops, analyse it with AI models, and recommend actions to improve health and yield.
  - **Example**: A team of students develops a system to detect pest infestations early.
- **Managing Waste in Schools:**
  - Design an AI-based waste segregation system using sensors and image recognition to promote recycling.
  - **Example**: Smart bins that identify and sort recyclable materials.

6.3 AI Competitions and Hackathons

Purpose: Foster innovation and collaboration by engaging students in competitive, team-based activities.

- **School-Level Hackathons:**
  - Students form teams to solve a given problem using AI, such as designing a solution to monitor air quality in classrooms.
  - **Example**: A team creates an AI-powered air quality tracker using IoT sensors and a mobile app.
- **Community AI Challenges**:
  - Students collaborate with local leaders to address larger community problems, such as predicting water shortages or improving traffic flow.

- o **Example**: A competition where students develop an app to map water resources and identify shortages.
- **National/International AI Events**:
  - o Participation in broader AI competitions like Kaggle challenges or Google Science Fair, helping students showcase their talents on a larger platform.

Figure 6.1: Collaborative AI Projects with Community Stakeholders

6.4 Collaborative Group Activities

Purpose: Build teamwork and problem-solving skills through AI-driven group tasks.

- **Designing AI Tools for Businesses**:
  - o Groups develop chatbots or recommendation systems to help local shops manage customer inquiries or inventory.
  - o **Example**: A team creates an AI-powered pricing tool for a local vegetable market.
- **Community AI Projects**:
  - o Students collaborate to analyse community health data (e.g., Diabetes) and create awareness campaigns.
  - o **Example**: A group designs an app to monitor vaccination coverage in their village.

6.5 Creative AI Projects

Purpose: Spark creativity and innovation by using AI for artistic and imaginative activities.

- **AI-Powered Art and Music**:
    - Use tools like Deep Art or AI Music to create AI-generated artwork or music compositions. <u>Muse net only gives theory to create music so related to AI music which can create music.</u>
    - **Example**: A student uses AI to compose a school anthem or design posters for school events.
- **AI in Storytelling**:
    - Use AI tools like ChatGPT to co-create stories or develop interactive storytelling apps.
    - **Example**: A project where AI generates alternate endings to popular fairy tales.

6.6. Real-World Applications of AI Projects

Purpose: Connect AI learning to practical use cases with tangible community benefits.

- **Water Quality Testing:**
    - Students use IoT sensors and AI to test and report the quality of water sources in their community.
    - **Example**: A system that flags unsafe water and suggests purification methods.
- **Renewable Energy Monitoring:**
    - Students develop AI systems to track the efficiency of solar panels in their school or village.
    - **Example**: An app that shows daily energy production and usage.

- **Healthcare Support**:
  - AI projects that assist in health diagnostics, like a tool to identify common symptoms of illnesses.
  - **Example**: A chatbot that suggests basic remedies for common health issues and recommends visiting a doctor if needed.

6.7 Practice Session

This session provides exciting opportunities to apply AI concepts in real-world scenarios. Engage in beginner projects, problem-solving challenges, and creative activities to explore the potential of AI in your school and community.

Exercise 1: Beginner-Level AI Projects

Task:

Choose one of the following projects to start your AI journey:

1. **Create a Chatbot**
   - Use **Scratch**, **Python**, or **Dialog flow** to design a chatbot that answers questions or provides helpful information.
   - Example: Build a chatbot that helps students find library books or school schedules.
2. **Analyse Weather Data**
   - Collect local weather data and analyse it using **Google Colab** or **Microsoft Excel**.
   - Example: Predict rainfall and suggest activities based on weather conditions.
3. **Build a Simple AI Model**
   - Use platforms like **Teachable Machine** to create a recognition model.
   - Example: Train a model to identify different types of leaves or school supplies.

Exercise 2: Problem-Solving Challenges

Task:

Work individually or in teams to tackle a community or school issue:
1. **Improve School Attendance**
   o Analyse attendance data with AI tools to identify patterns of absenteeism.
   o **Example**: Create a system to notify parents of their child's attendance status.
2. **Monitor Crop Health**
   o Simulate collecting crop data and use an AI tool to detect pest infestations.
   o **Example**: Propose actions to improve crop health using analysed data.
3. **Manage Waste in School**
   o Design a system that uses image recognition to sort waste into recyclable categories.
   o **Example**: Build a "smart bin" for your school.

Exercise 3: AI Competitions and Hackathons

Task:

Participate in a team-based AI activity:
1. **School-Level Hackathon**
   o Form teams to design a solution using AI for a given challenge.
   o **Example**: Build an AI tool to monitor air quality in classrooms.
2. **Community AI Challenge**
   o Collaborate with local leaders to solve a community problem.
   o Example: Create a water resource mapping app to address shortages.
3. **National AI Competitions**
   o Research and join national or international AI events.
   o Example: Prepare for a Kaggle competition by analysing sample datasets.

Exercise 4: Collaborative Group Activities

Task:

Work in small groups to complete an AI-driven project:

1. **Design AI Tools for Businesses**
   - Develop tools like chatbots or recommendation systems for local shops.
   - **Example**: A chatbot that helps a grocery store manage customer inquiries.
2. **Community AI Projects**
   - Analyse data and create tools to support community health or education.
   - **Example:** Design an app to track vaccination rates and send reminders.

Exercise 5: Creative AI Projects

Task:

Unleash your creativity with AI:

1. **AI-Powered Art or Music**
   - Use tools like **DeepArt** or AI Music to create artwork or compose music.
   - **Example**: Design posters for a school event or compose a theme song.
2. **AI Storytelling**
   - Co-create a story using tools like **ChatGPT**.
   - **Example**: Write alternate endings for famous fairy tales or invent a new adventure.

Exercise 6: Real-World Applications of AI

Task:

Create practical AI tools for meaningful community impact:

1. **Test Water Quality**
   - Use AI tools to analyse water safety in your area.
   - **Example**: Design a system that flags unsafe water sources and suggests solutions.

2. **Monitor Renewable Energy**
   - Track the efficiency of solar panels with AI.
   - **Example:** Build an app to visualize energy production and usage.
3. **Support Healthcare**
   - Create tools that assist with health monitoring or basic diagnostics.
   - **Example:** A chatbot that recommends remedies for common symptoms.

Exercise 7: Investigative Task

Topic: Testing Drinking Water Quality Using IoT Sensors and AI

Instructions:

- **Collect Water Samples**:
  - Gather drinking water samples from five different sources in your area (e.g., tube well, pond, river, well, tap water).
- **Analyse Using IoT Sensors**:
  - Use IoT-enabled water quality sensors to measure the **salt value** in parts per million (ppm) for each water sample.
  - Record the following values (for example):
    - Sample 1: **100 ppm**
    - Sample 2: **250 ppm**
    - Sample 3: **20 ppm**
    - Sample 4: **90 ppm**
    - Sample 5: **450 ppm**

Figure 6.2: Screen short of an IoT Device

- **Research WHO (World Health Organisation) Guidelines**:
  - Use the prompt:
    "Salt's parameter values of the water samples are: 100 ppm, 250 ppm, 20 ppm, 90 ppm, and 450 ppm. Are these values suitable for human health according to the recommendation of WHO?"
  - Query LLMs or online resources to determine whether these values fall within the WHO recommended TDS limits for safe drinking water.
- **Evaluate Suitability:**
  - Compare the measured values against the WHO standard for drinking water' salt values.
  - Identify which water sources are suitable for drinking and which may pose health risks.
- **Write a Report:**
  - Prepare a 3-page report summarizing your findings.
  - Include the following sections:
    - **Introduction**: Overview of water quality testing and the importance of salt level monitoring.
    - **Methodology**: Steps for collecting water samples and using IoT sensors for analysis.
    - **Findings**: Present the salt values and their comparison with WHO standards.
    - **Discussion**: Interpret the results and highlight possible health implications of unsuitable water sources.
    - **Recommendations**: Suggest measures to improve water quality or alternative sources for safe drinking water.
- **Prepare a Presentation:**
  - Create a 10-minute presentation summarizing the task and findings.
  - Use visuals, such as charts or graphs, to illustrate the TDS levels and their suitability for human health.

Deliverables:
1. **Written Report:**
   o A detailed 3-page document containing your analysis and conclusions.
2. **Slide Deck:**
   o A concise presentation (6-8 slides) highlighting your findings, including visuals.

Goal:

This exercise allows you to explore how IoT sensors can monitor water quality and evaluate drinking water's suitability based on WHO standards. It enhances your understanding of practical IoT applications and promotes awareness of public health standards in your community.

Chapter 6 focuses on practical engagement with AI through hands-on projects, problem-solving challenges, and creative exercises. It introduces beginner-level AI activities, such as building chatbots, analysing data, and creating AI models, designed to help students understand and apply AI concepts effectively. The chapter emphasizes collaborative projects like hackathons, community-driven initiatives, and competitions that encourage teamwork, innovation, and real-world problem-solving. By connecting AI applications to everyday life and societal challenges, it empowers students and educators to develop critical thinking, creativity, and technical skills while making meaningful contributions to their communities.

Chapter 7:
Empowering Teachers to Lead AI Initiatives

Empowering Teachers to Lead AI Initiatives focuses on equipping educators with the knowledge, skills, and resources needed to effectively integrate AI into classrooms and mentor students in AI-driven projects. This chapter provides guidance on teacher training, ethical AI practices, and continuous professional development to ensure educators are confident in fostering innovation. By empowering teachers as leaders in AI education, schools can create a collaborative and future-ready learning environment that benefits both students and communities.

7.1 Training Teachers in AI Basics

Purpose: Equip teachers with the foundational knowledge and skills needed to integrate AI into their teaching and guide students effectively.

- **Introduction to AI Concepts:**
  - Provide a simple and practical understanding of key AI concepts, such as machine learning, natural language processing, and computer vision.
  - Use teacher-friendly tools and platforms like Teachable Machine, Scratch, or Google Colab to demonstrate AI in action.
- **Hands-On Training Programs**:
  - Conduct workshops and online courses to train teachers on how to use AI tools in the classroom.
  - Topics include creating AI-driven lesson plans, using data for personalized teaching, and running AI lab projects.
- **AI for Classroom Management**:
  - Teach teachers to use AI tools like Edmodo and ClassDojo for monitoring student performance and engagement.
  - **Example:** AI systems to analyse attendance and identify students who may need additional support.

7.2 Teaching AI Ethics and Safety

Purpose: Ensure teachers understand the ethical implications of AI and can guide students in using AI responsibly.

- **Understanding Ethical AI Use**:
  - Introduce topics such as bias in AI algorithms, fairness, and inclusivity.
  - **Example:** Discuss how AI might favour certain groups over others and how to address these biases.
- **Promoting Data Privacy and Security:**
  - Teach teachers how to educate students about protecting personal data when using AI tools.
  - Demonstrate how to select AI platforms that prioritize security and ethical standards.
- **Responsible AI Practices:**
  - Encourage teachers to emphasize the importance of transparency, accountability, and sustainability in AI projects.
  - **Example:** Projects that highlight the environmental impact of AI systems and propose eco-friendly alternatives.

7.3 Continuous Professional Development

Purpose: Help teachers stay updated with the latest advancements in AI and ensure they can continually improve their skills.

- **Access to Online Resources**:
  - Share a curated list of AI courses, webinars, and certifications tailored for educators.
  - Recommended platforms include Coursera, edX, and Khan Academy for AI-specific modules.

- **Teacher Communities and Networking**:
    - Encourage teachers to join AI-focused groups and forums where they can exchange ideas, resources, and experiences.
    - **Example:** Local or national teacher networks for collaborative learning on AI integration.
- **Incentivizing Skill Development**:
    - Provide recognition for teachers who complete AI training programs, such as certificates or opportunities to lead school-wide AI initiatives.
- **On-Site and Peer Mentorship**:
    - Establish a mentorship system where experienced teachers guide others in integrating AI into their classrooms.
    - **Example:** Teachers who excel in AI projects can hold monthly peer-led workshops.

7.4 Facilitating AI Integration Across Subjects

Purpose: Empower teachers to incorporate AI into diverse subject areas beyond STEM, making learning more engaging and relevant.

- **Interdisciplinary Applications**:
    - Demonstrate how AI tools can enhance learning in arts, literature, social sciences, and sports.
    - **Example:** Using AI to analyse historical trends in social studies or create AI-generated artwork in visual arts.
- **AI-Driven Teaching Aids**:
    - Provide resources for integrating AI into lesson plans, such as using chatbots for interactive Q&A sessions.
    - **Example:** AI tools to generate quizzes and track student performance automatically.

7.5 Supporting Teachers in Leading AI Projects

Purpose: Enable teachers to mentor students in AI-driven projects and competitions.

- **Guiding Students in Problem-Solving**:
    - Provide a framework for teachers to help students identify community challenges and develop AI solutions.
    - **Example:** Assisting students in creating an AI-powered app to track community health trends.
- **Organizing AI Events**:
    - Support teachers in hosting school-wide AI hackathons, innovation fairs, or inter-school AI competitions.
    - **Example:** A teacher-led project fair showcasing student innovations, such as AI tools for climate monitoring.
- **Collaborating with External Experts**:
    - Connect teachers with AI professionals and organizations for guest lectures, workshops, or mentorship.
    - **Example:** Invite an AI expert to discuss real-world applications of AI during a school event.

7.6 Encouraging Teacher-Led AI Initiatives

Purpose: Inspire teachers to take leadership roles in promoting AI awareness and adoption in schools and communities.

- **Developing School-Wide AI Strategies**:
    - Encourage teachers to design an AI integration roadmap for their schools, outlining goals and steps for implementation.
    - **Example:** A plan to establish an AI lab within three years and integrate AI into 50% of lessons by year two.
- **AI Awareness Campaigns:**
    - Teachers can lead efforts to educate parents and the community about the benefits of AI in education and daily life.

- o **Example:** Organize an AI Awareness Day to showcase how AI improves learning and problem-solving.
- **Collaborating with the Community:**
  - o Guide teachers in working with local leaders and organizations to use AI for community development projects.
  - o **Example:** Teachers lead a project where students use AI to monitor water quality in the village.

7.7 Practice Session (Explore Appendix-B for lesson plan)

Exercise 1: Training in AI Basics

Activity: Exploring AI Concepts

- Use a teacher-friendly tool like **Teachable Machine**, **Scratch**, or **Google Colab** to complete a beginner AI project.
- **Example:** Train a simple image recognition model to identify different types of classroom objects (e.g., books, pencils, laptops).

Reflection:

- How could you use this tool to enhance your lesson plans?
- Which AI concept would you like to explore further?

Exercise 2: Teaching AI Ethics and Safety

Activity: Identifying Bias in AI

- Review a sample dataset (e.g., a dataset for predicting test scores) and discuss potential biases in the data.
- **Example** Questions:
  - o Are all groups of students equally represented?
  - o How could bias in the data affect AI predictions?

Activity: Data Privacy Scenarios

- Discuss a scenario where student data is collected by an AI tool. Develop strategies to:

1. Protect student privacy.
2. Obtain consent from parents or guardians.
3. Ensure the AI tool complies with ethical standards.

Reflection:
- How will you teach students about ethical AI use and data privacy?

Exercise 3: Continuous Professional Development

Activity: Exploring AI Resources
- Choose one AI training course or webinar from platforms like **Coursera**, **edX**, or **Khan Academy**.
- Complete a module and write a short summary of what you learned.

Activity: Building an AI Teacher Network
- Join an AI-focused teacher group (online or offline) or create one for your school.
- Discuss how AI tools are being used in classrooms and share teaching strategies.

Reflection:
- What benefits do you see in collaborating with other teachers on AI initiatives?

Exercise 4: Facilitating AI Integration Across Subjects

Activity: Interdisciplinary AI Applications
- Choose a subject you teach and brainstorm how AI could enhance the learning experience.
- **Examples:**
  - In literature: Use AI to analyse writing styles in famous novels.
  - In sports: Use AI to track and improve student performance in physical activities.

Activity: Creating an AI-Driven Lesson Plan
- Use an AI tool like ChatGPT or an educational platform to design an interactive lesson.
- **Example:** Create an AI-generated quiz or use a chatbot for Q&A sessions during class.

Reflection:
- How did using AI tools change the way you approached lesson planning?

Exercise 5: Supporting AI Projects

Activity: Guiding Student Projects
- Mentor a group of students in identifying a community issue and brainstorming an AI solution.
- **Example:** Help students create an AI-powered app to monitor air quality around the school.

Activity: Organizing an AI Event
- Plan a small-scale AI hackathon or project showcase for your school.
- **Example:** Challenge students to design AI tools for improving school recycling programs.

Reflection:
- What challenges did you face in mentoring students, and how did you address them?

Exercise 6: Encouraging Teacher-Led AI Initiatives

Activity: Developing an AI Integration Plan
- Work with fellow teachers to create a roadmap for integrating AI into your school.
- Include:
  - Short-term goals (e.g., setting up an AI workshop).
  - Long-term goals (e.g., establishing an AI lab).

Activity: Leading an AI Awareness Campaign

- Organize an AI Awareness Day for students and parents.
- **Example:** Demonstrate AI tools like chatbots, data analysis platforms, or AI-generated art.

Reflection:

- How can AI initiatives transform teaching practices in your school?

Exercise 7: Collaboration with External Experts

Activity: Guest Speaker Session

- Invite an AI professional to speak to your class or school. Plan questions and topics to discuss with them, such as:
    - Real-world AI applications.
    - Career opportunities in AI.

Activity: Building Partnerships

- Collaborate with a local organization to design a project where students use AI to address a community challenge.
- **Example:** Monitor energy usage in a local community centre using AI tools.

Reflection:

- How can external collaborations enhance the learning experience for both teachers and students?

Exercise 8: Investigative Task for Teachers

Topic: How can I use LLMs for Student Task Assessment and Feedback?
Instructions:

- **Research Using AI Tools:**
    - Use various large language models (LLMs), such as ChatGPT, Bard, or similar platforms, to explore how LLMs can assist in assessing student tasks and providing meaningful feedback.
    - Compare the responses to understand different approaches and methodologies.

- **Provide Context for Your Research:**
  - Define specific assessment criteria (e.g., clarity, creativity, grammar, problem-solving).
  - Outline the desired feedback model (e.g., rubric-based, personalized comments, improvement suggestions).
  - Specify the target audience (e.g., school students, university students, or adult learners).
- **Test Practical Scenarios:**
  - Input examples of student tasks (e.g., essays, problem-solving exercises, or creative writing) into LLMs.
  - Analyse the quality, accuracy, and relevance of the feedback provided by each tool.
- **Write a Report:**
  - Prepare a concise report (approximately 3 A4 pages) summarizing your findings.
  - Include the following sections:
    - **Introduction**: Overview of the importance of AI in student assessment and feedback.
    - **Methodology**: Describe the LLMs used and the criteria for evaluation.
    - **Findings**: Present the feedback variations from different LLMs and assess their strengths and limitations.
    - **Discussion**: Analyse the suitability of LLMs for different types of assessments and contexts.
    - **Recommendations**: Suggest best practices for integrating LLMs into student assessment processes.
- **Prepare a Presentation**:
  - Create a 10-minute presentation summarizing your findings.
  - Use slides to highlight key points, such as:
    - Assessment criteria.
    - Feedback examples from LLMs.

- Comparison of different LLMs' performance.
- Recommendations for implementation.

Deliverables:

1. **Written Report:**
   - A 3-page document detailing the research, findings, and recommendations.
2. **Slide Deck:**
   - A 10-minute presentation with visuals, feedback examples, and analysis.

Goal:

This exercise will help you understand how LLMs can be used to assess student tasks and provide feedback effectively. By exploring variations in feedback models and testing practical scenarios, you will gain insights into how these tools can enhance the teaching and learning process.

Chapter 7 emphasizes equipping teachers with the knowledge, skills, and resources to integrate AI into classrooms effectively, fostering innovation and mentoring students in AI-driven projects. It provides strategies for training teachers in AI basics, ethical AI practices, and continuous professional development, ensuring they remain confident and future ready. By enabling teachers to lead AI initiatives, schools can cultivate a collaborative and innovative environment that benefits both students and communities.

Chapter 8:
Building a community of AI Innovators

Building a Community of AI Innovators emphasizes the importance of collaboration among students, teachers, families, and local leaders to create a thriving ecosystem of AI-driven innovation. This chapter explores strategies for engaging the entire community in AI projects, sharing success stories, and fostering partnerships that address local challenges. By cultivating a culture of innovation and teamwork, this chapter aims to inspire individuals to use AI as a tool for meaningful social and economic transformation.

8.1. Engaging Families and Local Leaders

Purpose: Strengthen community involvement by creating a collaborative environment where families, local leaders, and schools work together to leverage AI for local challenges.

- **Involving Families in AI Projects**:
  - Encourage parents and guardians to participate in school AI initiatives, such as supporting students' AI-driven agricultural or health projects.
  - **Example:** Parents collaborate with students to implement an AI-based irrigation system to optimize water usage in farming.
- **Workshops for Families:**
  - Organize community workshops to educate families on the practical benefits of AI in daily life, such as financial planning, health monitoring, or energy conservation.
  - **Example:** A workshop showing families how to use AI apps to budget household expenses.

- **Local Leaders as Champions:**
  - Involve village leaders in AI-driven projects to ensure alignment with community needs and goals.
  - **Example:** A local leader supports a student project to use AI-powered drones for crop monitoring and pest control.
- **Community Problem-Solving Forums:**
  - Host regular forums where families and leaders can share challenges and brainstorm solutions using AI tools.
  - **Example:** A meeting to discuss how AI can help monitor and improve water quality in the community.

8.2 Showcasing Success Stories

Purpose: Inspire others by highlighting the achievements of students, teachers, and community members in using AI to create innovative solutions.
- **Student-Led Innovations:**
  - Share case studies of students who developed AI solutions for local challenges.
  - **Example:** A student project that used AI to predict crop diseases and shared insights with local farmers, resulting in increased yields.
- **Teacher Contributions:**
  - Highlight teachers who successfully integrated AI into their classrooms and mentored student projects.
  - **Example:** A teacher who guided students to build an AI-powered chatbot to answer frequently asked questions about their school.
- **Community-Wide Impact Stories:**
  - Document how community-led AI initiatives improved living conditions, such as reducing waste or increasing renewable energy adoption.
  - **Example:** A community project using AI to optimize solar energy usage, reducing electricity costs by 20%.

- **Social Media and Local Media Campaigns:**
    - Use digital platforms to share success stories widely, encouraging other schools and communities to adopt similar initiatives.
    - **Example:** Posting before-and-after results of a water quality project powered by AI on social media.

8.3 Collaborating Across Communities

Purpose: Create a network of AI innovators by fostering connections between schools, families, and local leaders from different communities.

- **Inter-School Collaborations:**
    - Organize AI projects that bring together students and teachers from neighbouring schools to work on joint solutions.
    - **Example:** A group project between two schools to develop an AI-based weather forecasting system for local farmers.
- **Community Networking Events:**
    - Host events where communities can share best practices, tools, and AI project outcomes.
    - **Example:** A regional AI fair showcasing projects like AI-powered waste management systems or health monitoring tools.
- **National AI Competitions:**
    - Encourage schools and communities to participate in national-level AI challenges to gain recognition and access to resources.
    - **Example:** A nationwide AI hackathon focusing on solving rural challenges using AI-driven innovations.
- **Building Long-Term Partnerships:**
    - Partner with NGOs, government agencies, and tech companies to provide funding, mentorship, and technical support for AI projects.
    - **Example:** A tech company sponsors AI labs in schools and offers free training for teachers and students.

8.4 Encouraging Peer-to-Peer Learning

Purpose: Empower students and teachers to learn from one another, fostering a culture of shared knowledge and collaboration.

- **Student-Led Workshops:**
  - Senior students mentor juniors by teaching basic AI concepts and tools.
  - **Example:** A workshop where older students demonstrate how to create an AI chatbot using Scratch.
- **Teacher Learning Circles:**
  - Teachers from different schools meet regularly to share AI teaching strategies and resources.
  - **Example:** A group of teachers develops a shared repository of AI lesson plans and projects.
- **Community Knowledge Sharing:**
  - Involve families and local leaders in sharing traditional knowledge that can be enhanced using AI.
  - **Example:** A family shares insights on water conservation, and students use AI tools to develop a predictive water usage model.

8.5 Promoting a Culture of Innovation

Purpose: Foster a mindset of curiosity, experimentation, and resilience in tackling challenges through AI.

- **Innovation Challenges:**
  - Organize regular innovation competitions where students propose AI-powered solutions to community problems.
  - **Example:** A challenge to design an AI system for tracking waste collection efficiency in the village.
- **AI Idea Boards:**
  - Set up digital or physical boards in schools and communities where people can suggest problems and ideas for AI solutions.
  - **Example:** A suggestion to use AI to predict flood risks and notify villagers in advance.

- **Encouraging Risk-Taking:**
    - Teach students and teachers that failure is part of the learning process in AI innovation.
    - **Example:** A failed project to develop an AI-driven irrigation system becomes a learning experience for creating a more effective solution.

8.6 Practice Session

This session focuses on fostering collaboration among students, teachers, families, and local leaders to create impactful AI-driven solutions. Through these activities, participants will engage in practical, community-cantered AI projects and build a thriving ecosystem of AI innovators.

Exercise 1: Engaging Families and Local Leaders

Activity: Community Brainstorming Forum
- Host a forum where families, students, and local leaders identify key challenges in the community.
- Use AI tools to brainstorm potential solutions.

Steps:
1. Divide participants into groups and assign each group a challenge (e.g., water management, waste recycling, or crop health).
2. Discuss how AI can address these challenges.
3. Present your ideas to the larger group.

Reflection:
- What role did families and leaders play in developing solutions?
- How can their involvement strengthen the project?

Exercise 2: Collaborating Across Communities

Activity: Joint AI Project with a Neighbouring School
- Partner with another school to work on a shared AI project.

Steps:
1. Identify a common challenge (e.g., flood prediction, waste management).
2. Use tools like **Google Colab** or **Scratch** to develop a collaborative solution.
3. Share progress through regular virtual or in-person meetings.

Reflection:
- What did you learn from collaborating with another school?
- How did different perspectives improve the project outcome?

Exercise 3: Encouraging Peer-to-Peer Learning

Activity: Student-Led AI Workshop
- Senior students host a workshop for juniors, teaching them how to use a basic AI tool.

Steps:
1. Choose an accessible tool like **Teachable Machine** or **Scratch**.
2. Create a simple project (e.g., an AI model to recognize objects or create a chatbot).
3. Guide juniors through the steps to complete the project.

Reflection:
- How did mentoring others deepen your understanding of AI?
- What feedback did you receive from juniors?

Exercise 4: Promoting a Culture of Innovation

Activity: Innovation Challenge
- Organize a competition where students propose AI-powered solutions for community problems.

Steps:
1. Identify specific problems (e.g., reducing traffic congestion, improving energy usage).
2. Form teams to brainstorm and design AI-driven solutions.
3. Present ideas during a school or community event.

Example Projects:
- An app to track and manage household energy consumption.
- An AI model to predict crop diseases based on weather patterns.

Reflection:
- How did the challenge encourage creative thinking and problem-solving?
- What lessons were learned from the proposed solutions?

Exercise 5: Building Long-Term Partnerships

Activity: Partner with Local Organizations
- Collaborate with NGOs, government agencies, or businesses to fund and support an AI project.

Steps:
1. Identify a local partner (e.g., a tech company, agricultural cooperative).
2. Present a project idea and discuss how they can support it (e.g., funding, mentorship, resources).
3. Implement the project and share results with the community.

Reflection:
- How did the partnership enhance your project?
- What future opportunities do you see for similar collaborations?

Exercise 6: AI Idea Board

Activity: Suggest and Vote on AI Ideas
- Set up a digital or physical board for students, teachers, and community members to post AI project ideas.

Steps:
1. Collect ideas (e.g., AI-powered flood monitoring, waste sorting systems).
2. Review and vote on the most impactful or feasible ideas.
3. Form teams to work on the top-voted idea.

Reflection:
- How did the idea board encourage participation from everyone?
- What makes an idea suitable for implementation?

Exercise 7: Sharing Knowledge and Insights

Activity: Organize a Community AI Fair
- Plan a fair where students showcase AI projects to families, local leaders, and other schools.

Steps:
1. Set up booths or digital presentations for each project.
2. Include hands-on activities where visitors can try AI tools.
3. Collect feedback from attendees to improve future projects.

Reflection:
- How did the fair engage the community in AI innovation?
- What new ideas or opportunities arose from the event?

Exercise 8: Investigative Task (Collaborative)

Topic: How can we measure the water parameters of fish farms, and can AI guide us in addressing unusual parameter values?

Instructions:
- **Research Using AI Tools**:
  - Use various large language models (LLMs), such as ChatGPT, Bard, or other AI platforms, to explore how water parameters in fish farms can be measured and monitored.
  - Investigate how AI tools can assist in interpreting these parameters and suggesting corrective actions when values deviate from optimal ranges.
- **Provide Context for Relevance:**
  - Include details about your specific location, type of fish farm, and commonly farmed species (e.g., tilapia, catfish).
  - Reference local fisheries documents, guidelines, or traditional knowledge to contextualize the AI suggestions.

- **Identify Key Water Parameters:**
  - Research common water parameters critical for fish health, such as:
    - Temperature
    - pH levels
    - Dissolved oxygen (DO)
    - Ammonia levels
    - Salinity
  - Explore how IoT sensors and AI-powered systems can monitor these parameters in real-time.
- **Analyse AI's Role:**
  - Use prompts to ask LLMs how AI can help interpret unusual parameter values (e.g., high ammonia levels) and recommend corrective measures.
  - Compare responses from different LLMs and identify the most practical or innovative solutions.
- **Write a Collaborative Report:**
  - Prepare a detailed 3-page report summarizing your findings, with contributions from team members.
  - Include the following sections:
    - **Introduction**: Importance of water quality in fish farming and the role of AI in monitoring.
    - **Methodology**: How LLMs and local knowledge were used for research.
    - **Findings**: Key insights on water parameter measurement tools and AI-driven solutions.
    - **Discussion**: Practical applications of AI in your local context, challenges, and limitations.
    - **Recommendations**: Suggestions for implementing AI-based monitoring systems in fish farms.
- **Prepare a Team Presentation:**
  - Create a 10-minute collaborative presentation.

- Use slides to include:
  - An overview of water parameters and their importance.
  - Examples of AI tools and their applications.
  - Recommendations for local implementation.

Deliverables:
1. **Written Report:**
   - A 3-page collaborative document summarizing your findings and team discussions.
2. **Slide Deck:**
   - A 10-minute presentation with visuals, graphs, and examples of AI applications.

Goal:

This exercise aims to explore how AI can improve water quality management in fish farming by identifying unusual parameter values and suggesting corrective measures. Through teamwork and contextual research, participants will understand the potential of AI to enhance local aquaculture practices and address real-world challenges.

Chapter 8 emphasizes the importance of fostering a collaborative and inclusive community of AI innovators to drive meaningful change. It highlights how students, educators, and professionals can work together on AI projects, share knowledge, and develop solutions to address global and local challenges. The chapter provides strategies for building innovation hubs, hosting AI-focused events, and creating mentorship opportunities to nurture creativity and teamwork. By cultivating a supportive environment, it inspires individuals to leverage AI for social impact, technological advancement, and the collective betterment of society.

Chapter 9:
Ethical Considerations in AI

As AI continues to shape the educational landscape, understanding its ethical implications is crucial. This chapter explores how schools, families, and communities can ensure AI is used responsibly, inclusively, and securely.

9.1 Fairness and Inclusivity in AI

Understanding Bias in AI

AI systems often reflect the biases present in the data used to train them. These biases can result in unequal or unfair outcomes, such as favouring certain demographics over others.

- **Examples in Education**:
    - Admission or grading systems powered by AI could unintentionally favour students from certain backgrounds.
    - Language barriers in AI tools might exclude non-native speakers.
- **Key Questions to Ask:**
    - Is the training data diverse and representative?
    - Are the AI tools reviewed regularly for unintended biases?

Promoting Equitable Use

- **Accessibility**: Ensure that AI tools are designed to meet the needs of all students, including those with disabilities.
- **Cultural Sensitivity**: AI should respect cultural differences and avoid stereotypes.
- **Collaboration**: Involve diverse groups of educators, students, and community members in the design and deployment of AI solutions.

Best Practices

- Conduct regular audits of AI systems to identify and mitigate bias.
- Provide training for educators on how to use AI inclusively.

9.2 Data Privacy and Security

How to Protect Personal Data in AI Systems?

- **Understanding Data Collection**:
    - AI systems in schools may collect sensitive information, such as grades, behaviour records, and health data.
    - It's crucial to understand what data is being collected and how it is used.
- **Key Challenges:**
    - Unauthorized access to student data.
    - Lack of transparency in data storage and usage.
    - Potential misuse of data by third-party AI vendors.

Protecting Personal Data

- **Data Minimization**: Collect only the data that is absolutely necessary for the AI to function.
- **Encryption**: Use strong encryption methods to protect data during storage and transmission.
- **Access Control**: Restrict access to sensitive data to authorized personnel only.
- **Parental and Student Consent**: Obtain clear consent before collecting personal data.

Creating a Secure Environment

- Regularly update and patch AI systems to prevent cyber threats.
- Conduct security audits to identify vulnerabilities.
- Educate students and parents about online safety and data privacy.

9.3 Responsible AI Development

Encouraging Ethical Decision-Making

- **Accountability**: Developers and educators must take responsibility for the outcomes of AI systems.
- **Transparency**: AI tools should clearly explain their functions and decisions. Students and teachers should understand how the system works and why it makes certain recommendations.
- **Human Oversight**: Always include a human in the loop to monitor and guide AI decisions, especially in sensitive areas like grading or behaviour monitoring.

Avoiding Misuse of AI

- **Examples of Misuse**:
  - Using AI for excessive surveillance, which can erode trust and create stress among students.
  - Exploiting AI-generated insights for commercial gain at the expense of student well-being.
- **Promoting Ethical AI:**
  - Incorporate ethical guidelines into AI education programs for students and teachers.
  - Foster discussions about the potential risks and benefits of AI in the classroom.

Framework for Responsible AI

- **Fairness**: Ensure that AI benefits everyone equally.
- **Accountability**: Assign responsibility for AI outcomes.
- **Transparency**: Make AI processes clear and understandable.
- **Ethical Design**: Prioritize student well-being and safety in all AI tools.

9.4 Practice Session

Exercise 1: Exploring Fairness and Inclusivity in AI

Activity: Identify and Discuss Bias in AI
- Choose an AI tool or system commonly used in education (e.g., a language learning app, a grading system, or a recommendation engine).
- Analyse how it could unintentionally favour or exclude certain groups of students (e.g., based on language, region, or access to technology).

Steps:
1. Write a list of questions to evaluate fairness in the AI tool, such as:
   - Does the tool work equally well for students with disabilities?
   - Does it account for different languages or cultural contexts?
2. Share your findings with the class and discuss ways to improve fairness in the system.

Exercise 2: Safeguarding Data Privacy and Security

Activity: Create a Data Privacy Checklist
- Work in small groups to design a checklist for protecting personal data in an AI system used at school.

Steps:
1. Research key principles of data privacy (e.g., data minimization, encryption, parental consent).
2. Include questions such as:
   - Is the data encrypted during storage and transfer?
   - Are students and parents informed about how their data is used?
   - Who has access to the data?
3. Present your checklist to the class and apply it to evaluate a fictional or real AI tool.

Exercise 3: Responsible AI Development

Activity: Role-Playing Ethical AI Decisions
- Simulate the role of an AI developer tasked with creating a system for schools.
- Scenario: Your AI system is designed to monitor student attendance.

Steps:
1. As a group, list potential ethical challenges, such as:
   - Should the AI notify parents automatically, or allow teacher oversight?
   - How will you ensure the system is unbiased toward specific groups?
2. Write a short ethical policy for your system, focusing on fairness, accountability, and transparency.
3. Present your ethical policy to the class and explain how it addresses the challenges.

Exercise 4: Case Study Analysis - Ethical AI in Action

Activity: Investigate Real-World AI Ethics Cases
- Choose a real-world example of an AI system that faced ethical challenges (e.g., bias in hiring algorithms or misuse of facial recognition in schools).

Steps:
1. Research the case and summarize:
   - The purpose of the AI system.
   - The ethical issues that arose.
   - How the issues were addressed (or not).
2. Write a short reflection on what lessons schools can learn from the case.

Exercise 5: Creative Ethics Campaign

Activity: Design an Awareness Poster or Video
- Work individually or in groups to create a poster, infographic, or short video promoting ethical AI use in schools.

Steps:
1. Include topics like:
   - Why fairness and inclusivity matter.
   - How to protect personal data.
   - The importance of responsible AI development.
2. Use AI tools (e.g., Canva, ChatGPT) to design your materials.
3. Share your campaign with classmates and display it in your school.

Exercise 6: Interactive Debate - Is AI Always Fair?

Activity: Participate in a Classroom Debate
- Debate Topic: "Can AI systems ever be completely fair and unbiased?"

Steps:
1. Form two groups—one supporting the idea and the other opposing it.
2. Research examples of bias and fairness in AI systems.
3. Present arguments and listen to counterarguments.
4. Reflect on the discussion and write a short paragraph summarizing your perspective.

Exercise 7: Create an Ethical AI Framework

Activity: Design a Framework for Ethical AI Use in Your School
- Work as a class to create guidelines for how your school can adopt AI tools responsibly.

Steps:
1. Identify key principles, such as:
   - Ensuring AI tools are inclusive and accessible.

- Protecting student data.
- Providing transparency about how AI tools work.
2. Compile these principles into a "School Ethical AI Policy."
3. Discuss how these guidelines can be implemented in real scenarios.

Exercise 8: Investigative Task

Topic: What are the Digital Scams in Society, and How Can They Be Mitigated?

Instructions:

- **Research Using AI Tools:**
    - Use various large language models (LLMs), such as ChatGPT, Bard, or other similar platforms, to explore the types of digital scams prevalent in society and effective strategies to mitigate them.
    - Compare the responses to gain diverse perspectives and identify the most relevant insights.
- **Provide Context for Relevance:**
    - Include specific details based on your location, region, or country to tailor the findings.
    - Consider areas of interest, such as financial scams, phishing, identity theft, or social media fraud, to make the research more targeted.
- **Identify Key Types of Digital Scams:**
    - Research common digital scams, such as:
        - Phishing emails and websites.
        - Social engineering tactics (e.g., impersonation scams).
        - Online shopping fraud.
        - Fake investment schemes.
        - Malware and ransomware attacks.
    - Explore how these scams impact individuals, businesses, and communities in your region.

- **Analyse Mitigation Strategies**:
  - Use prompts to ask LLMs how these scams can be mitigated through:
    - Public awareness campaigns.
    - Improved cybersecurity practices.
    - Implementation of robust laws and regulations.
    - Adoption of AI tools to detect and prevent fraudulent activities.
- **Write a Report:**
  - Prepare a concise report (approximately 3 A4 pages) summarizing your findings.
  - Include the following sections:
    - **Introduction**: Overview of digital scams and their societal impact.
    - **Types of Scams**: Description of key scams and their relevance to your region.
    - **Mitigation Strategies**: Practical approaches to reduce the risks of digital scams.
    - **Discussion**: Challenges in implementing these strategies and the role of AI in combating scams.
    - **Recommendations**: Suggestions for individuals, businesses, and governments to improve digital safety.
- **Prepare a Presentation:**
  - Create a 10-minute presentation summarizing your findings.
  - Use slides to include:
    - An overview of digital scams.
    - Examples and case studies relevant to your context.
    - Mitigation strategies and recommendations.

Deliverables:
1. **Written Report:**
   - A 3-page document summarizing the research, findings, and recommendations.
2. **Slide Deck:**
   - A 10-minute presentation with visuals, examples, and key points for discussion.

Goal:

This exercise aims to explore the types and impacts of digital scams while identifying strategies to mitigate them. By contextualizing the findings and using AI tools for analysis, participants will gain a deeper understanding of how to enhance digital security in their communities.

Ethical considerations are central to ensuring that AI supports education in a positive and inclusive way. By promoting fairness, safeguarding data privacy, and encouraging responsible development, schools and communities can maximize the benefits of AI while minimizing its risks. This requires ongoing collaboration between educators, developers, students, and families to create a future where AI empowers everyone.

Chapter 10:
AI for National and Global Growth

AI for National and Global Growth highlights how AI innovations can drive economic development, solve critical societal challenges, and position communities on the global stage. This chapter explores the role of AI in advancing national priorities such as education, healthcare, agriculture, and sustainability while aligning with global goals like the UN's Sustainable Development Goals (SDGs). By connecting local AI solutions to broader contexts, this chapter demonstrates the potential for AI to foster inclusive growth and contribute to a brighter, tech-enabled future.

10.1. Connecting Local Innovations to National Goals

Purpose: Demonstrate how small, community-driven AI solutions contribute to broader national priorities and global sustainability efforts.

- **Aligning with Sustainable Development Goals (SDGs)**:
  - Highlight how AI initiatives address key SDGs such as quality education, good health, sustainable cities, and climate action.
  - **Example**: An AI-powered waste management system aligns with SDG 12 (Responsible Consumption and Production) by promoting recycling and reducing waste.
- **Solving National Challenges through Local AI Solutions:**
  - Show how local projects can scale to address challenges like agricultural inefficiency, healthcare access, and digital literacy on a national level.
  - **Example**: An AI-based crop monitoring project implemented in a village could be scaled up to improve agricultural productivity across the country.

- **Showcasing Impact at National Forums:**
  - Encourage communities to present their AI projects at national innovation fairs and conferences to gain recognition and funding.
  - **Example**: A school demonstrates its AI-powered flood prediction model at a national disaster management forum.
- **Data-Driven Policy Recommendations:**
  - Use insights from community AI projects to inform government policies and strategies.
  - **Example**: Data from AI-driven water quality monitoring projects helps shape national clean water policies.

10.2 AI as a Driver of Economic Growth

Purpose: Emphasize how AI contributes to economic development by creating jobs, enhancing productivity, and fostering innovation.

- **Improving Efficiency in Key Sectors**:
  - Agriculture: AI tools optimize resource usage, increase crop yields, and reduce costs.
  - Healthcare: AI enables early diagnosis, personalized treatment, and efficient patient management.
  - Education: AI platforms enhance learning outcomes, addressing skill gaps in the workforce.
  - Industry: AI-powered automation increases efficiency and reduces operational costs in manufacturing and logistics.
- **Creating AI-Related Job Opportunities**:
  - New roles such as data scientists, machine learning engineers, and AI ethics consultants emerge as AI adoption grows.
  - **Example**: A community AI lab trains students for future jobs in AI-based agriculture and healthcare.

- **Empowering Entrepreneurs and Startups**:
  - AI lowers barriers to entry for new businesses by providing tools for market analysis, customer engagement, and product innovation.
  - **Example**: A startup uses AI to develop a mobile app that connects rural farmers to urban markets, boosting income and reducing dependency on intermediaries.
- **Fostering Global Competitiveness:**
  - By developing AI skills, communities can contribute to a tech-savvy workforce, positioning the nation as a hub for AI talent and innovation.
  - **Example**: A government initiative supports AI learning in schools to create a pipeline of skilled professionals for global tech companies.

10.3 Building a Future-Ready Workforce

Purpose: Prepare students and communities with the skills needed to thrive in an AI-driven world, ensuring long-term economic resilience.

- **Integrating AI into Education and Vocational Training**:
  - Develop AI-based curricula that teach problem-solving, critical thinking, and technical skills.
  - **Example**: Vocational programs train youth in AI-driven industries like renewable energy management and digital marketing.
- **Upskilling and Reskilling Programs:**
  - Offer ongoing training for adults to adapt to changing job markets due to AI advancements.
  - **Example**: Workshops on AI-powered tools for local businesses help entrepreneurs modernize their operations.
- **Promoting Lifelong Learning:**
  - Encourage a mindset of continuous learning to keep up with advancements in AI and digital technologies.
  - **Example**: Online learning platforms like Coursera and Khan Academy offer free or affordable AI courses.

10.4 Scaling AI Innovations Globally

Purpose: Position local AI projects as scalable models that can be replicated in other regions and countries to address global challenges.

- **Global Sharing of Best Practices:**
    - Collaborate with international organizations to share successful AI solutions developed by communities.
    - **Example**: A water conservation AI model from Bangladesh is adapted for drought-prone areas in Africa.
- **Participation in International Competitions:**
    - Encourage schools and communities to showcase their AI projects at global platforms like Google Science Fair or UNESCO Innovation Challenges.
    - **Example**: Students present an AI-powered renewable energy monitoring system at an international energy summit.
- **Attracting International Partnerships and Investments:**
    - Highlight the success of AI projects to attract funding and technical support from global organizations.
    - **Example**: A global tech company sponsors the scaling of a community AI initiative to monitor climate change impacts.
- **Contributing to Global AI Development:**
    - Encourage local participation in global AI research, ensuring diverse perspectives and equitable growth.
    - **Example**: Students and teachers collaborate on an AI research project with international universities to study the impact of AI on rural education.

10.5 Promoting Ethical AI Practices for National Growth

Purpose: Ensure the responsible and equitable use of AI to drive sustainable development and inclusive growth.

- **Teaching AI Ethics**:
  - Emphasize fairness, transparency, and accountability in AI development.
  - **Example**: Projects that address algorithmic bias and promote inclusivity in AI systems.
- **Encouraging Data Privacy and Security:**
  - Develop guidelines for schools and communities to handle data responsibly.
  - **Example**: Community-led initiatives to educate citizens about securing their digital information.
- **Sustainable AI Development:**
  - Promote the use of eco-friendly AI technologies that minimize energy consumption and environmental impact.
  - **Example**: AI models optimized to reduce computational power requirements in resource-limited settings.

10.6 Practice Session

Practice Session Tasks: AI for National and Global Growth

These practice tasks are designed to help students, teachers, and communities understand the transformative potential of AI in driving national and global development. Participants will work on real-world applications, explore economic opportunities, and learn to scale innovations responsibly.

Exercise 1: Connecting Local Innovations to National Goals

Activity: Map Local AI Projects to National Priorities
- Identify an AI project in your school or community (e.g., an AI-powered irrigation system or health monitoring tool).
- Map its contributions to national goals or SDGs.

Steps:
1. Research relevant national priorities (e.g., agriculture efficiency, clean water, disaster management).
2. Create a visual map showing how the AI project aligns with one or more SDGs.
3. Present your findings to classmates, highlighting the potential for scaling the project nationally.

Reflection:
- How can your AI project make a larger impact if implemented nationwide?
- What challenges might arise in scaling the project?

Exercise 2: AI as a Driver of Economic Growth

Activity: Sector-Specific AI Solutions
- Choose a sector (e.g., agriculture, healthcare, education, or industry) and design a simple AI-powered solution to enhance productivity.

Examples:
- For **agriculture**: An AI system that predicts optimal planting times based on weather data.
- For **healthcare**: A chatbot that provides basic health advice for rural communities.

Steps:
1. Identify a challenge in the chosen sector.
2. Develop a plan for how AI can address this challenge, including tools or data needed.
3. Share your solution with the group and discuss its feasibility.

Reflection:
- How does your solution improve efficiency or create economic opportunities?
- What skills or resources would be required to implement it?

Exercise 3: Building a Future-Ready Workforce

Activity: Upskilling for the AI Economy
- Create a learning pathway for someone in your community (e.g., an unskilled worker) to acquire AI-relevant skills before working abroad.

Steps:
1. Identify the target skills (e.g., communication, digital literacy, or technical skills).
2. Use free AI-powered platforms like **Duolingo**, **Coursera**, or **LinkedIn Learning** to create a step-by-step training plan.
3. Present the plan to your classmates and suggest ways to encourage participation.

Reflection:
- How can AI tools make skill-building accessible to unskilled workers?
- What are the key challenges in promoting lifelong learning in your community?

Exercise 4: Scaling AI Innovations Globally

Activity: Design a Global Scaling Strategy
- Choose an AI project from your school or community and plan how it could be scaled to another country.

Examples:
- A **flood prediction system** in Bangladesh adapted for flood-prone regions in Southeast Asia.
- A **crop disease detection app** scaled to other agricultural economies.

Steps:
1. Research the target region's challenges and resources.
2. Develop a strategy for adapting and implementing your AI solution, considering cultural and technical factors.
3. Create a short presentation or poster showing your scaling strategy.

Reflection:
- What additional resources (e.g., funding, partnerships) would be needed to scale your project globally?
- How can international collaboration improve the solution?

Exercise 5: Promoting Ethical AI Practices for National Growth

Activity: Develop an AI Ethics Policy
- Work in teams to create ethical guidelines for using AI in national development projects.

Topics to Address:
1. **Bias**: Ensure AI systems are inclusive and fair to all demographics.
2. **Data Privacy**: Protect personal data collected through AI tools.
3. **Sustainability**: Minimize the environmental impact of AI systems.

Steps:
1. Write a one-page policy document outlining your guidelines.
2. Include examples of how these guidelines could apply to specific AI projects (e.g., a national healthcare chatbot).
3. Share and discuss your policy with the group.

Reflection:
- Why is it important to prioritize ethics in AI development?
- How can these policies ensure sustainable and equitable growth?

Exercise 6: Encouraging International Collaboration

Activity: Join a Global AI Challenge
- Work in teams to prepare for a hypothetical global AI competition, such as a UNESCO or Google Science Fair challenge.

Challenge Example:
- Design an AI tool to address climate change in low-income countries (e.g., a tool for predicting droughts or optimizing renewable energy usage).

Steps:
1. Research a real-world problem that aligns with the competition's theme.
2. Use online tools like **Google Colab** to develop a prototype or concept for your solution.
3. Write a proposal explaining your solution's impact, scalability, and feasibility.

Reflection:
- How does participating in global competitions benefit your school and community?
- What support would you need to turn your concept into reality?

Exercise 7: Community AI Impact Showcase

Activity: Host an AI Showcase Event
- Organize an event where students, teachers, and community members present their AI projects to local leaders and families.

Steps:
1. Set up booths or presentations for each project.
2. Include interactive demonstrations of AI tools.
3. Invite feedback from attendees to improve and scale projects.

Reflection:
- What did you learn from presenting your project?
- How can community feedback shape the future of your AI initiatives?

Exercise 8: AI-Powered Career Pathways

Activity: Career Planning with AI
- Use AI tools to explore future career opportunities related to AI and technology.

Steps:
1. Research career options in AI-driven industries like healthcare, agriculture, and manufacturing.
2. Use platforms like **LinkedIn Career Explorer** or **ChatGPT** to identify skills needed for these roles.
3. Create a career development plan, including courses or certifications to pursue.

Reflection:
- How can AI tools help individuals navigate career pathways?
- What role does lifelong learning play in building a future-ready workforce?

Exercise 9: Investigative Task

Topic: "Many people from low-income countries (e.g., Bangladesh) go abroad to work without adequate skills. How can AI tools help them develop their skills, such as communication?"

Instructions:

1. **Research Using AI Tools:**
   - Use various large language models (LLMs) to explore different responses to this prompt. Examples include ChatGPT, Bard, or similar AI tools.
   - Investigate how these tools can assist unskilled workers in developing essential skills, with a focus on communication and other job-related competencies.

2. **Contextualize Your Research:**
   - Incorporate details relevant to your location, region, and country to make the findings applicable to your specific environment.
   - Consider the types of work these individuals engage in abroad (e.g., construction, caregiving, hospitality) and tailor your research accordingly.

3. **Write a Report:**
   - Prepare a brief report (≈ 3 A4 pages) summarizing your findings.
   - Include key insights, specific AI tools or platforms that can help, and recommendations for practical implementation.
4. **Prepare a Presentation:**
   - Create a 10-minute presentation summarizing your findings.
   - Use slides to highlight key points, including the tools explored, examples of how they can be applied, and potential challenges or limitations.

Deliverables:
1. **A detailed 3-page report outlining:**
   - The potential of AI tools in skill development for unskilled workers.
   - Specific examples of AI tools (e.g., language learning apps like Duolingo, soft skill platforms like Udemy, or job-specific training tools).
   - Recommendations for implementing these solutions in your context.
2. **A slide deck for a 10-minute team presentation.**

Goal:
The exercise aims to deepen your understanding of how AI can address societal challenges and provide scalable solutions to improve skill development for unskilled workers from low-income countries. It also develops your ability to contextualize AI solutions and communicate findings effectively.

Chapter 10 explores the transformative potential of AI in driving national and global progress by fostering innovation, economic growth, and connectivity. It highlights how AI-powered tools can improve industries such as healthcare, agriculture, energy, and transportation, while addressing challenges like climate change and resource management. The chapter emphasizes the importance of international collaboration, data sharing, and equitable AI adoption to ensure inclusive and sustainable development. By showcasing real-world success stories and future opportunities, it inspires nations to leverage AI for building a more connected and prosperous global society.

Appendix – A

our examples are given here to explore AI-driven innovative project design and development. Guidance on addressing societal challenges can be obtained by using appropriate prompts with LLMs.

Project 1: Designing and Developing an LLM-Driven Chatbot with Contextual Knowledge

1. Define the Scope and Purpose:
- **Identify the core functionality:** What tasks should the chatbot perform? (e.g., customer service, information retrieval, task completion)
- **Determine the target audience:** Who will be using the chatbot? (e.g., customers, employees, students)
- **Set the level of sophistication:** How complex should the conversations be? (e.g., simple Q&A, open-ended discussions)

2. Select an LLM Model:
- **Choose a suitable model:** Consider factors like model size, cost, and performance. Popular options include GPT-3, GPT-4, and other language models from providers like OpenAI, Google AI, and Hugging Face.
- **Evaluate the model's capabilities:** Ensure it aligns with your chatbot's requirements, such as understanding context, generating human-like text, and handling complex queries.

3. Prepare and Process Data:
- **Gather relevant data:** Collect data from various sources, such as customer interactions, product documentation, and knowledge bases.
- **Clean and pre-process the data:** Remove noise, inconsistencies, and irrelevant information.
- **Create a knowledge base:** Organize the data into a structured format, such as a FAQ or a document database.

4. **Design the Chatbot's Architecture:**
   - **User Interface:** Design a user-friendly interface, either text-based or with a graphical user interface.
   - **Natural Language Processing (NLP) Component:** This component will handle natural language understanding and generation.
   - **Dialogue Management:** This component will manage the flow of the conversation, track the context, and determine the appropriate responses.
   - **Knowledge Base Integration:** This component will integrate the knowledge base into the chatbot's responses.

5. **Train the Model:**
   - **Fine-tune the LLM:** Train the LLM on your specific dataset to improve its performance on your tasks.
   - **Experiment with different techniques:** Consider techniques like prompt engineering, few-shot learning, and reinforcement learning to optimize the model's behaviour.

6. **Implement the Chatbot:**
   - **Choose a platform:** Select a platform like Dialogflow, Rasa, or a custom solution to deploy your chatbot.
   - **Integrate the LLM:** Connect the LLM to the platform and configure it to handle user queries.
   - **Test and iterate:** Continuously test and refine the chatbot to improve its performance and user experience.

Key Considerations for Contextual Knowledge:
   - **Contextual Memory:** Store and retrieve past conversations to provide more relevant and personalized responses.
   - **Knowledge Base Integration:** Incorporate a knowledge base to access and process information.
   - **Prompt Engineering:** Craft effective prompts to guide the LLM's responses and ensure they are relevant to the context.

- **Continuous Learning:** Regularly update the model with new data and feedback to improve its performance.

By following these steps and considering the key factors, you can develop a powerful LLM-driven chatbot that can provide informative and engaging interactions with users.

Project 2: Designing and Developing a Company-Specific LLM

Designing and developing a large language model (LLM) tailored to a specific company involves several key steps:

1. Define the Scope and Goals:
- **Identify Specific Use Cases:** Determine how the LLM will be used within the company. Will it be for customer service, internal knowledge base, content generation, or other applications?
- **Set Performance Metrics:** Establish metrics to measure the LLM's performance, such as accuracy, relevance, and coherence.

2. Data Collection and Preparation:
- **Gather Relevant Data:** Collect a diverse dataset that aligns with the company's specific domain and use cases. This might include internal documents, customer interactions, and public domain data.
- **Data Cleaning and Pre-processing:** Clean the data to remove noise, inconsistencies, and biases. Tokenize the text and consider techniques like data augmentation to increase the dataset's diversity.

3. Model Selection and Fine-Tuning:
- **Choose a Foundation Model:** Select a pre-trained LLM as a starting point. Popular options include GPT-3, Jurassic-1 Jumbo, or other state-of-the-art models.
- **Fine-tune the Model:** Train the model on the company's specific data to adapt it to the desired tasks and improve its performance. Use techniques like supervised fine-tuning, reinforcement learning from human feedback, and transfer learning.

4. Deployment and Integration:

- **Choose a Deployment Platform:** Select a platform like Hugging Face, AWS SageMaker, or Google Cloud AI Platform to deploy the LLM.
- **Integrate with Existing Systems:** Integrate the LLM into existing applications and workflows, such as customer service chatbots, internal search engines, or content generation tools.
- **API Development:** Create APIs to allow other applications to interact with the LLM.

5. Continuous Evaluation and Improvement:

- **Monitor Performance:** Continuously monitor the LLM's performance and identify areas for improvement.
- **Update the Model:** Retrain the model with new data and fine-tune it to address emerging needs and challenges.
- **Iterate and Refine:** Incorporate user feedback and insights to enhance the LLM's capabilities.

Additional Considerations:

- **Ethical Considerations:** Ensure the LLM is developed and used ethically, avoiding biases and harmful outputs.
- **Data Privacy and Security:** Protect sensitive data and comply with relevant regulations.
- **Cost-Effectiveness:** Consider the costs of training, deployment, and maintenance.
- **Scalability:** Design the LLM to scale as the company's needs grow.

By following these steps and considering these factors, companies can develop powerful LLMs that can significantly improve their operations and customer experiences.

Project 3: Design and develop an AI Tool to assess and provide feedback of students' assignments

Key steps involved in designing and developing such a tool:

1. Define the Core Functionalities:
- **Automated Grading:** The tool should be able to assess assignments based on predefined criteria, such as grammar, structure, content, and originality.
- **Personalized Feedback:** The AI should provide specific and actionable feedback, highlighting strengths and weaknesses.
- **Plagiarism Detection:** The tool should be able to identify instances of plagiarism by comparing the assignment to a vast database of text.
- **Bias Mitigation:** The AI should be designed to avoid biases in its assessments.

2. Data Collection and Preparation:
- **Collect a Diverse Dataset:** Gather a large dataset of student assignments, along with corresponding human-graded scores and feedback.
- **Data Cleaning and Pre-processing:** Clean the data to remove noise, inconsistencies, and irrelevant information.
- **Data Annotation:** Annotate the dataset with specific feedback points and grading criteria.

3. Model Selection and Training:
- **Choose a Suitable Model:** Select a language model, such as GPT-3 or BERT, that is capable of understanding and generating human language.
- **Fine-tune the Model:** Train the model on the prepared dataset, focusing on tasks like text summarization, sentiment analysis, and question answering.
- **Implement Feedback Generation:** Develop algorithms to generate specific and constructive feedback based on the model's analysis.

4. User Interface Design:
- **Intuitive Interface:** Design a user-friendly interface for both students and instructors.
- **Clear Feedback Presentation:** Present feedback in a clear and concise manner, highlighting key areas for improvement.
- **Integration with Learning Management Systems (LMS):** Integrate the tool with popular LMS platforms for seamless use.

5. Testing and Evaluation:
- **Pilot Testing:** Conduct pilot tests with a small group of students and instructors to gather feedback.
- **Evaluate Performance:** Assess the tool's accuracy, reliability, and user satisfaction.
- **Iterative Improvement:** Continuously refine the tool based on feedback and performance metrics.

By following these steps and leveraging advanced AI techniques, it's possible to develop an AI tool that can significantly enhance the efficiency and quality of student assessment and feedback. Would you like to delve deeper into a specific aspect of this process?

Project 4: Design and develop an AIoT (AI with IoT) driven system for fish farm monitoring, prediction and decision-making.

An AIoT-driven system for fish farm monitoring, prediction, and decision-making is a promising application of technology in aquaculture. Here's a breakdown of the key components and functionalities such a system could incorporate:

IoT Components:
- **Sensor Network:** Deploy a network of sensors to collect real-time data on various parameters like water temperature, pH, dissolved oxygen, turbidity, and nutrient levels.

- **Data Acquisition and Transmission:** Use IoT devices to gather sensor data and transmit it to a central cloud platform or server.

AI Components:

- **Data Processing and Analysis:** Use AI algorithms to process and analyse the collected data, identifying trends, patterns, and anomalies.
- **Predictive Modelling:** Employ machine learning techniques to forecast future conditions, such as potential water quality issues or disease outbreaks.
- **Decision Support Systems:** Develop AI-powered decision support systems to recommend optimal actions based on real-time data and predictions.
- **Computer Vision:** Utilize computer vision techniques to monitor fish health, behaviour, and growth.

Key Functionalities:

- **Real-time Monitoring:** Continuously monitor water quality parameters and fish health indicators.
- **Predictive Analytics:** Predict potential issues like water quality deterioration or disease outbreaks.
- **Automated Control:** Implement automated systems to adjust water parameters, feed distribution, and other factors based on AI-driven insights.
- **Alert Systems:** Trigger alerts to notify farmers of critical situations, such as low oxygen levels or disease outbreaks.
- **Optimization of Resource Usage:** Optimize the use of resources like water, feed, and energy.
- **Disease Detection and Prevention:** Implement AI-powered disease detection systems to identify and prevent outbreaks.

By integrating AI and IoT technologies, fish farmers can significantly improve efficiency, reduce costs, and enhance the sustainability of their operations.

Appendix – B

Prepare a Lesson Plan using ChatGPT and Copilot

The prompts:

1. Create a one-hour lesson plan for KS3 science based on the UK National Curriculum framework, covering the topic 'Atoms, Elements, and Compounds.' Include objectives, activities, resources, and assessment methods'; differentiated tasks or mini plenaries during the lesson.
   - a simple (Dalton) atomic model
   - differences between atoms, elements and compounds
   - chemical symbols and formulae for elements and compounds
   - conservation of mass changes of state and chemical reactions.

2. Create a PowerPoint presentation of the lesson plan including high quality images and embedded video links.

Lesson: Atoms, Elements, and Compounds
Lesson Title: Understanding Atoms, Elements, and Compounds
Duration: 1 hour
Year Group: KS3 (Key Stage 3 in UK)
Topic: Atoms, Elements, and Compounds

Learning Objectives:

By the end of the lesson, students will:
1. Understand the basic structure of an atom (Dalton's atomic model).
2. Differentiate between atoms, elements, and compounds.
3. Interpret chemical symbols and formulae for elements and compounds.
4. Apply the concept of conservation of mass in chemical reactions and changes of state.

Lesson Outline

1. Starter Activity (5 minutes)

- **Activity**: Students watch a 2-minute engaging video/animation on Dalton's atomic model.
- **Question**: "What is an atom? Why are atoms important?"
- Students write down their initial thoughts on sticky notes to gauge prior knowledge.

2. Introduction to Dalton's Atomic Model (10 minutes)

Teacher Explanation:

- Discuss the simple (Dalton) atomic model:
  - All matter is made of tiny particles called atoms.
  - Atoms of the same element are identical, while atoms of different elements are distinct.
- Use a visual aid/diagram on the board to represent Dalton's model.

Differentiation:

- **Challenge**: For advanced learners, briefly mention the limitations of Dalton's model compared to modern atomic theory.
- **Support**: Provide a labelled diagram of Dalton's atomic model for students who need additional help visualizing.

Mini-Plenary (2 minutes):

- Ask: "How did Dalton describe atoms of the same element?" Student's pair-share their answers.

3. Differences Between Atoms, Elements, and Compounds (15 minutes)

Teacher Explanation:

- Define: Atoms, elements, and compounds.
- Use practical examples:
  - **Element**: O_2 (oxygen gas).
  - **Compound**: H_2O (water).
- Display molecular models or animations to show the differences.

Activity: Sorting Task

- Students work in pairs to sort pictures or names into "Atoms," "Elements," or "Compounds."

Differentiation:
- **Challenge**: Ask advanced students to create their own examples of elements and compounds.
- **Support**: Provide a word bank with simplified definitions and examples for struggling students.

Mini-Plenary (3 minutes):
- Ask students to explain: "What is the difference between an element and a compound?" Volunteers share answers.

4. Chemical Symbols and Formulae (10 minutes)

Teacher Explanation:
- Introduce chemical symbols (e.g., H, O, Na) and formulae (e.g., H_2O, CO_2).
- Highlight the importance of subscript numbers in representing the quantity of atoms.

Activity: Match the Formula
- Students match chemical formulae to their names (e.g., H_2O = water, CO_2 = carbon dioxide).

Differentiation:
- **Challenge**: Ask advanced learners to write formulae for simple compounds when given the names.
- **Support**: Provide a table with some hints (e.g., H = hydrogen, O = oxygen).

Mini-Plenary (2 minutes):
- Quick quiz: Write the formula for "carbon dioxide" and "water" on mini whiteboards.

5. Conservation of Mass and Chemical Reactions (15 minutes)

Teacher Explanation:
- Explain conservation of mass: Matter is neither created nor destroyed in a chemical reaction.

- Use a simple demonstration: Combine vinegar and baking soda in a sealed bag and show no mass is lost.

Activity:
- Students solve a worksheet on balancing simple equations (e.g., H2 + O2 → H2O).
- **Extension**: Predict the products of a reaction when given the reactants.

Differentiation:
- **Challenge**: Advanced students balance slightly more complex equations (e.g., $CH_4 + O_2 \rightarrow CO_2 + H_2O$).
- **Support**: Provide partially completed equations for struggling students to finish.

Mini-Plenary (2 minutes):
- Ask: "Why is mass conserved in a reaction?" Discuss student responses.

6. Plenary (8 minutes)
- **Activity**: Exit Ticket:
    1. Write one thing they learned about atoms, elements, or compounds.
    2. Write one question they still have.
    3. Solve a quick riddle: "I am made of two hydrogen atoms and one oxygen atom. What am I?"

Differentiation:
- Provide sentence starters for struggling students (e.g., "One thing I learned is….").

Resources
- Sticky notes, molecular model kits or printed diagrams, matching cards, mini whiteboards, worksheet on balancing equations, and demonstration materials (vinegar, baking soda, sealable bag).

Note: We did not attach the ppt slides to avoid adding extra pages.

END

www.ingramcontent.com/pod-product-compliance
Lightning Source LLC
Chambersburg PA
CBHW071545220526
45469CB00003B/920